D0551375

Groovy Old Men

Groovy Old Men

A SPOTTER'S GUIDE

Nick Baker

ICON BOOKS

email: info@iconbooks.co.uk
www.iconbooks.co.uk

Sold in the UK, Europe, South Africa and Asia
by Faber & Faber Ltd, 3 Queen Square,
London WC1N 3AU or their agents

Distributed in the UK, Europe, South Africa and Asia
by TBS Ltd, TBS Distribution Centre, Colchester Road,
Frating Green, Colchester CO7 7DW

This edition published in Australia in 2008
by Allen & Unwin Pty Ltd,
PO Box 8500, 83 Alexander Street,
Crows Nest, NSW 2065

Distributed in Canada by
Penguin Books Canada,
90 Eglinton Avenue East, Suite 700,
Toronto, Ontario M4P 2YE

ISBN: 978-184831-020-9

Typeset in Minion by Ellipsis Books Limited, Glasgow

Printed and bound in the UK by CPI Mackays, Chatham ME5 8TD

Contents

CHAPTER ONE   *Groovy Old Men*   1

CHAPTER TWO   *History Men*   39

CHAPTER THREE   *Rock 'n' Roll*   71

CHAPTER FOUR   *Music 1 Politics 0*   109

CHAPTER FIVE   *Sex and Drugs*   147

CHAPTER SIX   *Stairlift to Heaven*   171

CHAPTER SEVEN   *The Future's So Bright*   211

CHAPTER EIGHT   *Three Funerals. No Weddings*   223

Acknowledgements   232

About the author

Nick Baker was born in 1952 and lives in London with his partner and two teenage sons. He has been a teacher, journalist, writer for teenagers, award-winning radio reporter and producer. He runs Testbed, a long-established radio and audio independent production company.

For Arthur, Gus and Sukey

CHAPTER ONE

Groovy Old Men

Wouldn't it be nice if we were older, then we wouldn't have to wait so long.

The Beach Boys, 'Wouldn't It Be Nice?'

I'm hanging about Balham tube, looking out for David's familiar silver Audi. I'm meeting him for lunch. He sneaks up behind me, like a kid with a surprise. He's on a bike. He makes out like it's no big deal. Maybe it isn't. 'It's hard to park near Balham tube, so I cycled', he explains. He launches into a description of a special bike he's adapted for his grand-children. It steers in the opposite way to the way you point it. He's always making stuff for his grandchildren. He's got ten; the youngest is two, the oldest 20-something. He's just taught the ten-year-old to juggle. Three balls, mind, proper. David learned to juggle in 1967. I ask him what's new. He's just seen Brian Wilson in concert, just seen the new Ian McEwan movie. He's reading that book about Wiki. He's just found out about lyrics sites on the internet. He moans about his job. He works for his son, a property developer. 'He tempted me back to work. I didn't want to. But I insisted on a company car and a credit card.' His job is to manage building and decorating projects in blocks of flats. He's a bit fed up with it. He has a moan about lazy builders, knocking off at 2pm on Fridays. Anyway, lately he hasn't been that busy.

He's immaculate, in black western shirt with pearly buttons, linen slacks, worn-looking loafers. Over lunch I see him eye one of my sausages. He's quite happy to eat off my plate as well as his, and without consulting orders a chocolate mousse, two spoons.

He's got polymyalgia rheumatica. We discuss whether cannabis would be preferable to steroids as a painkilling solution. He says his memory has been affected by smoking for over 50 years and he's stopped, though he had the greatest times when stoned. He says his wife says he gets garrulous and stupid when he smokes dope. Then he launches into a very detailed story from the seventies about his experiences in the antiques trade. He went to the first Glastonbury, in fact he worked at the first Glastonbury and has been to most of them since. He went to Joe Strummer's funeral. I reckon he's OK for a few bob. His favourite band at the moment is the Super Furry Animals. He's 77.

Ian, now 65, is a *Titanic* survivor. As a young teenager, he was one of the lucky ones who was allowed into the lifeboats, with his mother. A stern-faced man let them pass, after the usual 'women and children first' warning. His mother said he was fourteen. This was true. The stern-faced man was the actor Kenneth More, and the movie was *A Night to Remember*.

Ian, through no fault of his own, was a child actor, a main-stay of crowd scenes in fifties British movies. Kenneth More will reappear in this book, mainly as a manly icon of Groovy Old Men's youth. Ian will reappear too. In a later scene from a young life that sometimes seems like a Carry On film (he was a pupil in *Carry On Teacher*, by the way), Ian is unfairly accused of an interestingly glamorous sexual offence at the Windmill Theatre, famous for its all-nude review, and sacked from his electrician job there. I asked Hilary, a senior clinical psychologist, who now lives with Ian, what attracted her to him when they met five years ago: 'He was competent'. They're a dinner party 'match-made' couple. She had just ended a long-term relationship. He had just helped his youngest twin daughters deal with the death of their mother. He has seven children, all by this, his first wife. She was succeeded by a woman who left Ian for another woman. Then came Hilary, smitten by Ian's 'competence'.

'I was making a birthday cake in the shape of a boat, but I couldn't do the sails', she explains. 'Ian came up with some fantastic sails.' We're in their kitchen in Norwich. Upstairs, one of Hilary's daughters is studying for exams. They obviously like the same kind of busy domesticity. A short, light bicker breaks out about whether or not he shouts at old people blocking up the gangways in theatres. Ian can be outspoken. Actually, Hilary thinks he's fantastic with old people, presentable socially, as well as competent with children, boats, houses, electrics, food, friends, family and colleagues. Ian, now a musical instrument repairer/restorer, has had a diverse career, most of it on the craft side of theatre and television. He ventures the view that, in his boyhood, 1950s men mended cars with their fathers, many of whom were built along solid Kenneth More-type lines. Later, some of these same men, like Ian, became competent hands-on fathers, as well as able screwdriver operators. How this came about – the changes in family roles, greater opportunities for women, or just personal circumstance – may not matter. The important point is that competence isn't just a screwdriver thing. On the other hand, it's not a quality associated with infatuation. Ian and Hilary could have been friends, then, after the matchmaking. They look at each other and smile a bit. 'No, I don't think so', they say together. Hilary adds delicately, 'we were quite close quite quickly'.

Mike at 66: He gets up at 7am, does his exercises to iTunes or Wogan, makes and shares a cooked breakfast with his four-year-old, inspects his 60-acre garden, greets his 40-something second wife, browses some estate agents' details. He's looking to buy some properties away from the city and on higher ground. Very future-oriented, is Mike. He jumps into his car (the sensible Honda, not the 1952 Buick he lent to DJ Johnnie Walker for his wedding) and in 40 minutes he's upstairs at the award-winning Portobello Gold pub, which he's run for 22 years, negotiating over a new brand of organic lager. That's on a London day. On a home day he gets up, cooked breakfast, etc. etc., and plays a bit of guitar, reads, listens to music, rides the mower. He's getting an iPod for the mower. Little Feat is his favourite band.

Andrew has an infectious laugh. We're watching a DVD of his appearance on that little three-minute item after the *Channel Four News*. It's about compost, which is his favourite topic. When he first appears, a caption describes him as 'groundsman'. Not a bad description, but hardly an adequate one. For Andrew has been gardener, minicab driver, historian, sailor, farmer, TV researcher. He has met Jimi Hendrix, Princess Margaret and Winston Churchill and has had dealings with the Grateful Dead. He can build dry stone walls, shear sheep and navigate sea-going vessels. He's an expert on numerology and ley lines. For someone who was in at the start of the green movement, he doesn't bang on about it. Andrew is writing his autobiography and is saving all the good stuff for that, embarking on an anecdote then shutting up. But he has a generous nature and can't help telling stories. He lets slip that he helped install the toilets at the anti-nuclear camp on Greenham Common. 'Just the ladies.'

We're not laughing at that. We're laughing at Andrew's solemn Channel 4 announcement: 'I want my body to go on giving people pleasure after I am dead.' We're both fighting back the tears now. Andrew has been shipwrecked once and wrecked quite a lot. Although in our defence, our current laughter is fuelled by no more than the DVD, a glass of white wine and a pint of ginger beer shandy over lunch. Andrew is 73.

Terry, 70, plays a bit of guitar and does a bit of painting. He's a student of Salvador Dalí. He watches the builders putting up the kitchen extension and wishes he was doing it himself. He could have done it himself.

Ray Gosling, in white linen shirtsleeves, greets me from the tram in Nottingham, shouting up the hill like a kid. Come to think of it, he walks like a kid, a pugnacious head-down walking-up-the-hill walk, hands jammed in pockets, a walk that suggests a bit of Richmal Crompton's William Brown in it. Boyish is maybe a good description of Ray, with his spiky hair and blue eyes and sudden shoutiness. Unselfconcious is another. Uncompromising is another. That's possibly the secret of his success as a journalist. Says what he likes. He's 67. After his partner died he went bankrupt and moved into sheltered accommodation. That's where we're headed, although when you walk through Nottingham with Ray you stop every two minutes to say hello to people he knows, so it's slow going. A Tunisian, to whom Ray gives some friendly cheek about Ramadan, which is about to end. A pretty, blonde teenage girl. A bloke he teases about Bournemouth. Back in the lounge of what he calls the 'semi-sheltered' flats, Ray conducts a short argument with fellow residents about Elvis Presley, steals some milk, and we retreat to his rooms, which are piled high with papers, cuttings, articles, junk. The only neatness to be seen is the way he stores his notebooks, all identical and piled nicely high. Ray goes everywhere with a notebook and occasionally, unpredictably he jots something down. We talk for hours, and then we go to the pub. Ray pulls on a jacket. Paul Smith. Paisley lining, nicely cut. No contradiction about being 67 and wearing Paul Smith. Why should there be? I don't even ask. Besides, he and Paul are old mates, as it happens. It's not a big town, Nottingham.

After a long day, John drinks his first of two pints of lager in his local, the Portobello Gold. Every day, more or less, he has a couple of beers, three to five cigarettes, one joint. He confesses to be a bird-like eater, but he owes his continuing good health to a healthy lifestyle he led as a young man. John helps run an upmarket Portobello Road venue for fashion shows, antique fairs, book and record launches, art exhibitions. But his age – 70 in January 2008 – doesn't make him feel distant from his young colleagues and clients. In fact he feels closer to them than to most of the people his own age. (Except Mike, landlord of the Gold, who introduces him to me.) On this Monday in autumn the quiet Gold seems to be exclusively peopled with potential Groovy Old Men. The pub's full of pictures – Carl Perkins, Jimi Hendrix, the inevitable Stones with photographs by a Groovy Old Photographer, David Redfern. And the guy who brings us our plate of nachos, a bear-like white-bearded French-Mexican, seems like a candidate. 'Here, Pleasure', he says as he delivers the nachos. At least, that's what I think he says. It turns out that John's nickname is Pleasure. Judy Garland gave it to him.

Paul's a market trader, nearing 61. Touch of the Pete Townshends, if you ask me. White beard, sun hat, looks you in the eye, relaxed. He does T-shirts, novelty mainly. Captions like 'National Pornographic' channel, with two Rhinos having sex in silhouette. I buy 'I pood', a shirt with the image of a familiar silhouette of a man with white headphones, but he's not dancing, he's on the toilet. Paul does diamante T-shirts for the ladies, under what he calls the 'Primani' label. Primark prices, Armani style. I'm a bit worried, explaining my project to him, that he's too young to qualify. He could be my age (56). I'm relieved to hear he was born in 1947. He gets it straight away, and his initial reaction is a tribute to his female contemporaries. 'Women can still be a good shag at 60', he says.

Every so often, Don Wright, 62, spends a lot of time in cemeteries in Sheffield. It's a musical mission, in which a community theatre group puts on plays based on the stories of the dead. Musical interludes are provided by Don on bass and friends. Don's been retired from primary teaching since he was 50 and he's one of those *Daily Mail* villains, a 'liberal' school teacher from the 1960s, who put a lot of emphasis on children learning through creativity. He's the creative type himself. Singer-songwriter and lover of free jazz. On the count of ruining sixties kids' lives, he defends himself robustly, counting off his rebuttals on long guitar player's fingers. 'I also taught them reading, maths, tables, spelling.' One of his ex-kids – now a middle-aged big bloke with a Mohican who works in a Sheffield kids' playground – embarrassingly announced to his small customers that Mr Wright was 'the best teacher in the world'. I can imagine this to be true. Don looks like an older version of the comedian Tony Hawks and has the same kind of enthusiastic good humour, and the same thin-faced hooter as well. I was going to ask him a cemetery-related question about the prospect of death, but it somehow slipped my mind. But he did tell his mates in the local scratch folky pub band that he'd like to be playing there every week until – well until he couldn't do it any more, which I judge will be a long time.

This book explains what and who Groovy Old Men are, mainly by meeting them, looking at what they do, probing their histories and attitudes, and occasionally their music collections and wardrobes. And asking their wives nosy questions. (Jill, Don's wife, doesn't think Don looks like Tony Hawks.)

I'd advise anyone trying to use the book as a 'how to' not to. Those who come to be Groovy Old Men have done so effortlessly and unconsciously. It's a natural occurrence that doesn't happen to all men. Their grooviness, to a large part, has been ground by events. Their willingness to imbibe, accept, welcome and adapt the effects of the history that shaped their lives makes them Groovy. Their refusal to be categorised over the past 60 years has, paradoxically, linked them together. Any man who regards himself as a Groovy Old Man is, by definition, not one. However, you may be lucky enough to have one as a husband, father, brother, grandfather or secret lover. He may be a neighbour or friend, work in a local shop, clean your windows, be your landlord or write stuff for your newspaper. Or deliver it.

The mathematics are all rather pleasing. We're talking about stylish pre-boom babies made special by two kinds of sixties. The nineteen-sixties that helped shape them, and the bus-pass sixties they're now enjoying. Or may have already left. That's not to say Groovy Old Men should play the traditional 'young folk today, they don't know they're born' card as they board the bus: Ray Gosling pities the youth of today. Their version of youth pales in comparison with his memory of his:

'Oh: sorry for you. I look down on you from the upper deck on the bus – so you're into "your thing". Into your thing. Which is often something "they" have sold you. You have willingly let yourself buy what is marketed for you to think it is yours, and it isn't my dear. We set fashion. It was later that fashion and marketing caught on to our rebellion to sell a rebel look that's newly enslaved because you have to buy it. The punter has to buy the merchandise. We didn't buy. We created. We were never punters and never followed.'

Ray Gosling, writing in a new preface to his early autobiographical novel *Sum Total*, may be right about his own originality. He's a real creator, and *Sum Total* is one of the first British sixties books, first published when he was 21, in 1961, and probably the first British contemporarily created account of youth culture. But Groovy Old Men don't have to be youth-cult originals. Nor must they be Ray Gosling's fashion victims, the dedicated and now superannuated followers of fashion who 'have to have'. There are plenty of men in their 60s and 70s walking about in the latest trainers and trousers. It doesn't necessarily make them Groovy Old Men. Remember the tragic figure of Hugh Hefner, clinging to his combover and his swinging image? The harder you try, the harder it is to succeed.

I started out telling people that Groovy Old Men are 'more David Bailey than Peter Stringfellow'. I'm grateful to pop mag publisher David Hepworth who put me right by saying that

Stringfellow, now seen as a cross between Paul Daniels, Hugh Hefner and any member of Status Quo, a synonym for cheesy old lust, based his career on pioneering music clubs in his home town of Sheffield. If it wasn't for Stringfellow, there would be fewer Groovy Old Men there. The point being that Stringfellow does have some credibility, albeit mullet-occluded.

They've got to have shown discrimination – choosing and accumulating the best from the five decades they've lived through as adults. But in the opening decade of the 21st century, can these guys be, as it were, naughty in the noughties? Still get the kind of enjoyment they discovered in their youth?

A good place to look for them is where people go to relax and enjoy themselves: cinema queues, pubs, markets, airports, theatres, art galleries. Denims, trainers or walking shoes, back-pack, headphones, shades, a ponytail maybe, a book – they're slightly more visible than the standard old geezer we know and love to ignore, but self-effacing enough not to try to stand out in a crowd. Beware grey afros, too obvious youth-pants, excess jewellery, style-victim trainers, strange eyewear, the wearing of suits in inappropriate places, badges, evidence of retouched hair colour. Don't worry about poor colour co-ordination, less than perfect ironing, unmatched socks. Observe beards carefully. They can give out the wrong signals. Really you need to get these guys talking, or better still look at their music collection. So approach carefully, start to chat, and steal his iPod. He will see the humour of the situation, and in any event be too old to give chase. He'll also be insured by Saga, and see no contradiction between the Saga brand (for over-50s who can afford long holidays and are contemplating the purchase of elasticated trousers) and his devotion to free jazz or techno gypsy.

As you'll observe from the contents of the stolen MP3 player, it's not all cut and dried. There will, in this book as in life, be magnificent 100 per cent Groovy Old Men to meet, and there will be men with high GOM quotients, and lower GOM quotients. Very often, my researches start on the phone, which is probably not ideal. These guys can start out sounding promising. Here's a retired engineer, getting on for 70, water-colour painter, has come to amateur drama late in his life as well as doing a bit of set building. Sounds like my type of guy.

Crunch question. 'What kind of music do you like?'

'Light Opera ...'

I don't bother to do the next question about drugs or sex. This guy does have a traceable GOM count, albeit a comparatively low one. But he isn't my kind of guy after all. Or am I being unfair?

That's not to say Groovy Old Men are part of an airy-fairy subjective concept. They're almost definable. The trouble is, like all old people, they fall off the media radar once their spending power makes them not worth catering to. However, this is about to change, for economic if not cultural reasons.

While I'd strongly advise against using this book as a style bible, I think for older male readers not quite in the age group, it's perfectly legitimate to ask yourself or your loved ones whether you're likely to become one. Provided you have the sense of humour to laugh if they say no. And it's perfectly possible to be one and neither know nor care. It's just impossible to become one by trying. Sorry.

This is how it happened.

Early evening, after work, I was in a West End pub and my friend was handing out a bunch of tickets he'd acquired for a gig to a bunch of blokes selected for no other reason than they might like the band. Few of us knew each other; most of us were unlikely to meet again soon, so we weren't bothered with the niceties. My good friend Steve had organised it with the careless flair typical of a man who cares as much about music as he does about friendship.

So a mixed all-male group. In their 40s or 50s. A media johnny, a motorcycle courier, a bloke who runs a shop, a university lecturer maybe. Strangers, mostly. 'Hello, mine's a pint, how do you know Steve?' Steve being our ticketmaster. Master of minimal ceremonies. Etiquette somehow demanded we didn't ask each other about wives, work, stress level or kids. And that night I happened to be too knackered to be curious about my fellow gig-goers. And most men, in case you've not noticed, aren't given to personal questions, especially when there's something less interesting to talk about.

I am, however, a compulsive rubbernecker, byline spotter, TV credit watcher. I'm the one whose legs you crawl over at the end of a movie because I'm waiting for the names of the songs. I like to identify voice-overs on commercials. I'm a big Morse fan. Ken Morse. In the flesh I can identify minor celebs, people in the business, faces, voices, names at 50 paces. Naturally, having identified them, I ignore them.

So my radar flicked when this chap came into the pub. Tallish, slimmish, oldish. Leatherjacketish. Curly greying hair. Biggish nose. Earring. I'd say he was my age (56); no, older. A lot older, maybe. And there was something about him that sent me thumbing through my mental Rolodex. Actor? Journalist? Author? Movie producer? Something in the music industry? Artist? Charisma. This guy was somebody.

What really set my curiosity going was the mismatch between his clothes and demeanour and his, his ... damn, his *what*? I got a closer look. Then I got it. The mismatch was between his clothes, demeanour and his *age*. The nasty voice of prejudice whispered into my ear that he was too old to be wearing that jacket, to be having that hair, to be looking that spry. Unless he had earned the right to be like that in a proper job, worthy of my wrongheaded status consciousness. Big in the sixties, surely. Or seventies. Or maybe he had just some of that blowback style, a passive inhaler of someone else's fame or cool or talent. Casting agent. Book editor. Second unit director. Or maybe he was a top surgeon, former sports star, leading academic, retired. Because I had only two questions. Who is he? How old is he? I knew he was important. Not just generally, but important to me. In fact, I like to think of this as a 'eureka' moment, when the whole idea of Groovy Old Men fell into place.

It was on the tip of my tongue. Only my tongue was tied. And he was heading towards us. And if, as was entirely possible, he was going to be my mosh pit mate that night (in a middle-aged kind of way), then I had to know who and what this stylish-looking man of, what, 55 … 60 …? was – even if it meant not talking about it.

In the end I put myself out of my misery. Steve the ticket would know. Steve: 40-something, jazz expert, radio producer. Maybe there was a Steve connection. We weren't going to listen to jazz that night, but this man would look totally right in a line-up at Ronnie's, or being interviewed in the *Jazz on Three* studio.

By this time, the man in question is nearly upon us and I nudge Steve and semi-ventriloquically I say: 'Who *is* that?'

I was right about there being a Steve connection.

'That', says Steve, with admirable neutrality, 'is my dad.'

Steve's dad is the first Groovy Old Man I added to my 'I Spy' book. A former teacher, former cattery co-owner and once upon a time, yes, musician, he was at the time approaching 70 with effortless and anonymous grace.

Groovy Old Men represent a new phenomenon more real and more interesting than Grumpy Old Men. This idea depended on the theory that old men are grumpy because they are nearly dead and can't cope with a world that is leaving them behind. Ha ha, boom boom, end of story. And I hope end of mentions of the Grumps as well. Anyway, it should have been Grumpy *Nearly* Old Men, because it chose acceptable middle-aged men (Matthew Parris, Arthur Smith) rather than genuinely old men, who are unlikely to be featured sympathetically in light-hearted TV shows. Except Bruce Forsyth. Who is neither a grump nor a GOM.

Nor, incidentally, am I. Too young for both categories. But Steve's dad, born 1940-something, had an enviable and unique period in which to live, and seems to have absorbed it all. And as GOMhood beckons us, we in our 50s are looking out for role models for whom a condom tucked into the bus pass, or a motorcycle helmet in the pension queue, or an iPod with specially adapted headphones for the hard of hearing, or an item of arm-candy who will also help us cross the road won't look like a contradiction. This book is a bit of a guide. The common negative reaction I have had to my theory comes from younger men, particularly those in their 40s. They look carefully at me, ask me my age, we talk about the idea (I've been GOMhunting for two years and am always on the lookout) and they finally dismiss it as 'wishful thinking'. By which they mean, 'You don't think it's true, you *hope* it's true so you can age gracefully.' Or better still, disgracefully.

I agree very much that the idea involves optimism about men ageing. I hope it's true, not just so I can continue to live the life I please. Younger men tend to dismiss older men – or discrim-inate against them – so they can ease their own fear of death and comfort themselves that it's far away. I probably did. (Mind you, I hadn't read this book.) But there's a more general opti-mism, I hope, to be found in the idea. The men I'm talking to and about are the first, torchbearing generation and I predict, optimistically perhaps, that even the 40- and even 30-something doubting Thomases, Tobies and Tristrams who think it's all wishful thinking now will become Groovy Old Men one day.

Now, though, to a question that has to surface. Can women

16

become Groovy Old Men? Obvious, really. Women have always done old as if it were a decreasingly intense version of young. Even when, late in life, the hairstyles, colours and trappings of youthful sexual allure appear sometimes to be almost pantomimed, we accept it not as anachronism but convention.

The poet Jenny Joseph marked out some of this territory for women as early as 1961 with her immensely popular poem 'Warning':[1]

> When I am an old woman I shall wear purple
> With a red hat which doesn't go, and doesn't suit me.
> And I shall spend my pension on brandy and summer gloves
> And satin sandals, and say we've no money for butter.

By complete coincidence, I have just put the phone down after a conversation with a radio colleague about veteran DJ Annie Nightingale, now into her 60s and very much into drum 'n' bass. Dark-glassed, bleached-blonde, endlessly chatty, Annie's life-affirming but entirely individual outlook is not particularly purple, totally non-panto and not that unusual. Her love of music and extensive knowledge of it marks her out as a pretty good example of Groovy Old Man. She did, of course, get a head start as Britain's first female DJ.

'What about feisty women like … Germaine?' asks *Saga* magazine editor-at-large Emma Soames, dropping the 'Greer' because this is shop talk. Well yes, certainly, Germaine ticks

---

1 Once voted the UK's favourite.

a lot of the boxes and a few more besides. Note the 'feisty'. Women didn't get where they are today without a big helping of bolshy, unlike men. To men's shame, possibly.

And, of course, Annie and Germaine might qualify as Groovy Old Women. I don't claim that this category doesn't exist. Annie and Germaine might well be icons for it. But it isn't a category for which I want at the moment to provide a spotter's guide. It would be a lot more difficult. This is because not only have some women already staked out the territory of growing old disgracefully, they've also developed a *diverse* set of conventions for ageing – many but not all based on watered-down younger women's fashions and styles. It's a diversity that men largely lacked until now.

So, sit opposite an anonymised Germaine or Annie on a train and they'd be really difficult to categorise. Which is the DJ and which the academic? Either or both could be Member of Parliament, illegal immigrant, florist, software engineer, retired primary teacher, or full-time layabout.

I've chosen to write solely about men because they've kept quiet. Not diversified. Strategically, maybe. They've not been given to introspection. A good example comes from radio. In the 1980s BBC Radio 4 used to broadcast a weekly programme called *The Locker Room*, presented by Tom Robinson ('bisexual activist') and designed to discuss the sort of thing men discuss. Er, whatever that was. Or is. Not football, because they did that elsewhere on the radio. Or music. In fact my friend Steve with the Groovy old dad worked on it. But not for long. They took it off. *Woman's Hour*, meanwhile, has been a regular since 1946, its mission statement 'celebrating, entertaining and informing women'. I've just heard it: this morning, items on a theatre director, fish cookery and care of the elderly. Excellent stuff. My point is less about *Woman's Hour*'s longevity than it is about *The Locker Room*'s short-gevity.

Certainly the phenomenon of the Groovy Old Man has benefited, without aiming to do so, from women's history of inequality. In a sense, these men have 'got away' with things, been 'left to their own devices', and during the sixties they certainly benefited from an unequally large share of liberation, and they continue to benefit. Those men who have had long-standing relationships seem to have been indulged and in some cases forgiven by their wives and partners for the excesses of their past. This conversation seems to have repeated itself a number of times:

Me: So what was your wife/partner doing when you were doing all this?

Groovy Old Man: (sheepishly) Bringing up the children.

A female colleague, knowing I was writing on this subject, asked me whether you can be a Groovy Old Man and a sexist. My razor-sharp reply: Probably, but you'd have to feel at least a little bit guilty about it. To be honest, the reason my reply was razor sharp was because I had to spend about a week sharpening it.

Even now, I'm not sure that my razor-sharp reply was as good as her question. For months I have been carrying a mental image of the photographer David Bailey as a kind of icon for Groovy Old Men. Now in his 70s, the young Bailey broke into a world dominated by European upper-class gay men. He brought a famously frank heterosexual working-class cockney aesthetic to fashion and images of women. Reading the clippings, it becomes clear that a 21st-century interpretation of this process makes Bailey appear to be an unrepentant sexist. Or bad boy. Does this disqualify the much-married, occasionally grumpy-sounding Bailey from the status of Groovy Old Icon? Will it disqualify, say, Hanif Kureishi, as he approaches his older years? The answer is probably no.

Another female colleague explains that Bad Boys can by virtue of their badness be very attractive to women. A liking for Bad Boys is, she says, a phase that some women go through. So, colourful histories, even those that involve alleged negligence of partners, families and wives, do not disbar Bad Boys from becoming Groovy Old Men. In fact, they can sometimes help.

Another much-discussed icon is Bill Nighy, approaching the target age range but not there yet. Here we encounter the opposite phenomenon. Nighy has some of the same vintage attraction as Bailey, but Nighy's Mr Nice Guy. Why? Let's dispense with the clichés of little boys lost, of charming vulnerability and quintessential Englishness. For whatever reason, women fancy him as much as they fancy Bailey.

We learn three things here. One: Groovy Old Men have to have a hint of sexual attractiveness. To gauge this, the opinions of women have to be sought. (Although Groovy Old Gay Men are not banned from these pages.) Two: We're here to learn how to spot Groovy Old Men, not to judge them on moral grounds. Three: Let's not worry too much about celebs.

As comparators, they're very useful because their images are shared so widely, and part of the cost of celebrity is (famously) that they can't avoid scrutiny. To the spotter, they're great for target practice. But we only have public and possibly faulty perceptions of these guys. Which is why, with carefully chosen exceptions, I wanted to talk to civilians rather than celebs. Two ex-central heating engineers, a philosopher, two teachers, a couple of businessmen, a market trader and others. Just older blokes who I think are a bit Groovy.

I don't necessarily endorse the advantages that men have had over the past 50 years that have led some of them to this happy state. I simply observe it. And despite the Bad Boy phenomenon, long-lasting relationships seem to be a constant with these men. Although in the course of writing this book, one of my subjects, a man in his early 70s, split up from his long-term girlfriend, or wife, I can't remember which. I'm not sure he can.

So. Remaining Groovy or girly is a major preoccupation for women and has been since time immaterial. On the other hand, for a long time men were encouraged to mature. Even in his youth, David Niven always looked as if he had false teeth, yet this didn't detract from a perception of dashing good looks. Many men in this period seemed to have been born aged 40. Kenneth More. If men kept their youthful allure, they were labelled as homosexual. Dirk Bogarde.

I'd argue, then, that contrary to Shakespeare's seven ages, until the dawn of the time to which I'm referring (1956) there were only three stages of man: boy, man, old man. There were two rites of passage: from boy to man, short to long trousers.

This was for decency's sake. Hairy legs on a male child were unattractive and sent out the wrong signals. At the age of twelve, long trousers became the norm. From man to old man, false teeth. The change from real to false appears to happen overnight at an unspecified age (except in David Niven's case, who always had them, or so it seemed), around 60 usually. Perhaps improvements in dentistry should be included as influences. And it goes without saying that this is the first group of older people whose health has been looked after by the state. But these judgements are to do with all old *people*, and I'm classifying a very special sort. And until now old men got a particularly skewed and usually bad press. Try this at home: ask people to fill in the gap: '____old man'. You immediately get people filling in the blank with:

Dirty old man

This, according to my straw poll, is the favourite, initially bringing to mind two stereotypes: runny-eyed geezer too old to wash, and an ageing Lech. And I don't mean Walesa. Though he might well qualify. The 'Dirty Old Men' allegations are slanders, of course.

'… for the satirical rogue says here that old men have grey beards, that their faces are wrinkled, their eyes purging thick amber and plum-tree gum and that they have a plentiful lack of wit …' But Hamlet secretly agrees with the satirical rogue and old Polonius is a case in point. An ancient rambler, a bit of an old woman, a man whose untimely death doesn't matter, to Hamlet at least. And don't forget Hamlet's got a new stepdad, Claudius, who's shagging his mum.

So the epithet Dirty Old Man also evokes the universal Hamlet-related disgust that children have for their parents' (let alone grandparents') sexuality. It's well illustrated in the tortured relationship between Steptoe and Son. In one episode, to the intense disgust of Son, Steptoe starts 'courting'. The idea of an almost literally knackered World War One medal-jangling old man having a sex life, and the horror that his immature middle-aged child experienced as a result, touched a sensitive comic nerve, a sensitivity heightened by the unhygienic environment. (Episodes which feature Old Steptoe naked had the same effect.)

The protagonist in Lonnie Donegan's sixties hit 'My Old Man's a Dustman' is Steptoe's (and to an extent Claudius') natural musical counterpart. The fact that this is essentially a music hall song, sung by Lonnie Donegan[2] in the modern skiffle tradition, the council flat replacing the traditional poor-

2 Donegan was a deserving hitsmith and a worthy hero to GOMs and others. His fame had unexpected consequences. In the 1980s he suffered a heart attack. Tokyo newswires reported this and the Japanese stockmarket fluttered badly. This, however, was due to a Japanese/English confusion between Lonnie Donegan and Ronald Reagan. Donegan and Reagan had met 25 years earlier on American television. 'What is a Lonnie Donegan?' the confused president-to-be asked the audience of *The Perry Como Show*. Donegan's music conveniently bridges history. His first electric guitar was converted with the help of a second-hand pilot's throat microphone from a crashed Lancaster bomber.

house, helps point up the contrast. An unconscious anthem to the discontinuity of post-war masculinity. Innit?

In it, Donegan senior is, like Steptoe, a recycling industry worker, he famously wears a dustman's hat and 'gor blimey trousers', and is a local authority tenant. He too has a comedy-libido. Married at 86 ('it helps to pass the time'), he still has a roving eye. He accidentally misses a lady's bin one day and she chases after him, asking whether she's too late. 'No, jump up on the cart!', replies the old man.

Today, the notion of old men and sex is changing from within and without. Icons like Paul Newman and the Rolling Stones (and their PR people, photographers and management) cling bravely to the idea of their abiding sexual attractiveness, making it usefully acceptable for mere mortals to emulate. There's a growing acceptance for men to have children in later life. Viagra means old age isn't synonymous with impotence. The use of deodorants and other personal hygiene strategies is almost universal. Dirty Old Man is an outdated stereotype.

Silly/stupid old man

'Don't tell him Pike' is probably the greatest comic line in contemporary drama. The core joke of *Dad's Army* was that recruiting old men as a last line of defence against the Nazis was a very silly idea because these old men themselves tended towards silliness: incompetent, incontinent, pompous, doom-laden and crazily gung ho. These old fools wouldn't have stood a chance in combat against the U-boat captain they capture, who, despite being a prisoner, loftily demands – and gets – the name of the boy singing silly songs about the German army. And although it's a 60-something windbag of a bank manager played by Arthur Lowe who utters the line, 'Don't tell him Pike', the key silly old man is Lance Corporal Jones, survivor of the Great War and the Boer War, whose catchphrase about the 'fuzzy-wuzzies' was 'They don't like it up 'em.' Leaving aside the anachronism of 'fuzzy-wuzzy' (questionable even in 1968) and the irony of this decrepit specimen talking about the joy of shoving things 'up' people, this character works on another, funnier level. Dunn was 48 when he adopted the character. He'd already played a Somme survivor and SOM in a previous army comedy. As an even younger actor, he was the doddering dogsbody in *Bootsie and Snudge*, about a pair of former National Servicemen working in a gentlemen's club. The irony of a young man playing an older one adds depth to the character and the comedy. The message is that an old man as silly as this has to be played by a younger actor capable of pantomiming such advanced dotage.

Again, it's icons like Charles Saatchi, Rupert Murdoch, Alan Yentob even – ageing men who have kept hold of power and influence – who defeat the stupid old man stereotype. Again, the consistent if not increasing respect we have for ageing pop stars is also a powerful antidote.[3]

---

3 Mind you, there are some enjoyable paradoxes here. As I write, Michael Caine, 74, has just released an album of his favourite chill-out tracks, *Cained*. And Menzies Campbell has resigned from leadership of the Liberal Democrats, aged 66, under pressure about his age.

Wise old man/kind old man

This is best summed up in popular, mainly Christian, incarnations of God. Seen it all. Solemnly, quietly wise. Almighty (but not invisible) and generally benign. See also Father Christmas, Solomon, etc. Sadly, in the late 20th century it became a figure with waning popularity and meaning. We had relied on the experience and wisdom of old men in the First World War (epitomised by the Blimp character in the Powell and Pressburger classic *The Life and Death of Colonel Blimp*) and millions had been killed. That movie, released in 1943, incensed Churchill, aged 69, who felt himself undermined. Britain trusted Churchill to win the war, but not, aged 71, to lead the peace. They chose the more youthful 62-year-old Clement Attlee.

To find real value in the idea of wise old men, time for a time-trip to Plato, who between the ages of 67 and 82 devised *The Laws*, a blueprint for the conduct of a Utopian society he called Magnesia – whose milk, even to this day, is valued by old men and women, Groovy or otherwise. Plato's *Laws* have strict rules about age: men can't marry till 30 (women can marry between sixteen and twenty), you can't be the leader till you're 50, and, more significantly, 50 is the minimum age for qualifying to judge poetry competitions, while judges of contests involving musical soloists can be as young as 30.

Plato understood that age and cultural taste are linked. In his Ancient Greek poetic version of *The X Factor* (strictly speaking *The Chi Factor*), the panel is chosen for its maturity.

26

Wisdom in old men might be a prized attribute, but I'm content with mature cultural appreciation as a GOM ingredient. The GOM timeline has plenty on offer worth appreciating. Kenneth Tynan famously wrote: 'I could not love anyone who did not wish to see *Look Back in Anger*', of which more later. Irrespective of whether it's for books, plays, music, movies, drama, architecture, art: love is all you need. You can't be a philistine and a Groovy Old Man. Many GOMs are inventive or creative themselves. Many are enterprising, too. Those that are not have to appreciate creativity to qualify.

I'm indebted to Jeremy Baker (no relation) for bringing Plato's rules on poetry-judging to my attention. He reminds us that Tolstoy didn't learn to ride a bicycle until he was 67, after he finished writing *Anna Karenina*. Baker's book, *Tolstoy's Bicycle*, catalogues 7,500 achievements by the different ages of the people who achieved them. And the creative/inventive seem to do their best work in older age. At 60, architect John Nash starts work on plans for Regent Street. Casanova is 65 when he starts his diary. Goya's best work is achieved in his 60s. Torquemada starts his career as Inquisitor (a creative calling if ever there was one) in his 60s. Disraeli gears up to write his first novel at 66, the same age that Colonel Sanders has the bright idea of franchising his chicken restaurant to the nation. Sculptors, architects, novelists, musicians seem to keep running on creative energy. S.J. Perelman, the humorist, drives from Paris to Peking in an old MG at 74.

Baker, generous to a fault, says of his collation of ages and achievements that it has no specific point to make. 'The aim of the book is hypothesis generation, not hypothesis testing.' The hypothesis I gratefully generate is that this generation of old men has experienced an era of cultural cornucopia and if they're neither inventive themselves nor appreciative of others' invention in the true sense of the word, they're out on their ear.

In a way, this is one of the factors that distinguishes the GOM theory from run-of-the-mill 'Life begins at 60'-type propositions. Of course, oldies – men and women – can run corporations, get jobs at B&Q (though those orange Guantanamo Bay-style uniforms are draining of any natural colour in the complexion!) and join together to enjoy the benefits of improving lectures aboard the cruise ship *Saga*. Yes, their experience may make them wise and worthwhile, worthy of respect and equal opportunities. But it doesn't make them Groovy. The factors that make my men Groovy are the subject of this book and they are largely, but not entirely, historical.

First, though, there are some other old man images I want to deal with.

Old, Groovy and black/old, gifted and black/Old Man River

Louis Armstrong had a surprise hit with 'Hello Dolly' aged 64. But old black musicians have always enjoyed a special status, and it's intricately tied in to my GOM theories and quite hard to explain. I recently met acclaimed Rasta trombonist

Rico Rodriguez, born 1934 and the proud holder of two accolades. The first: he is an official Ian Dury[4] Reason to Be Cheerful, as I discovered when I was browsing lyrics sites for David Style, the man who invents trick cycles: 'Bantu Stephen Biko,/listening to Rico/Harpo, Groucho,[5] Chico'.

The second: Rico recently received an MBE for his services to music. The ever-inquisitive ska-fancier and ardent multiculturalist Prince Philip, Duke of Edinburgh, asked Rico: 'Do you ever take your hat off?'

Listening to Rico, it occurred to me that old black men have in the past century or so had an easier time being effortlessly Groovy and in so doing they inspired young, mainly white, men to become Groovy Old Men. The *coup de foudre* of hearing authentic black music for the first time plays a mythical part in many musicians' and Groovy Old Men's experiences, as you will see. It's the audio version of the Kennedy-assassination moment, with a more tasteful colour scheme. Mine is unremarkable and it happened in 1967. Passing my sister's bedroom I heard – on a cheap LP compilation that she had bought for the soul singers – Howlin' Wolf singing 'Smokestack Lightning'. Later my live music of choice was a succession of old black guys including Rev Gary Davis, Muddy Waters, Sonny Terry and Brownie McGhee,

4 Ian Dury was top of the list in a now abandoned chapter: Groovy Old Stiffs, about dead GOMs.
5 Groucho would have been number two.

Son House, and Chester Arthur Burnett aka Howlin' Wolf himself, a 6' 6" man-mountain who perhaps compromised his grooviness by suggestively dangling the mic chord from his crotch as he sang 'Wang Dang Doodle' to the Marquee Club audience in 1971.

Why in the seventies these old guys gave me the same thrill as that enjoyed by some of my contemporaries as they watched public-school-educated twenty-year-old acid-fuddled rock legends-to-be singing about knights and wizards is a mystery. It may well be that I liked the sense of history, tradition, commitment and authenticity they brought to the music, I dunno. I just say to myself, what a wonderful world. Maybe it's part of a long-held culturally conditioned set of responses that black men, irrespective of age, have always had credibility when it comes to playing rock 'n' roll and the blues, whereas old white men playing the same has until recently been looked at as weird. The Bonzo Dog Doo-Dah Band (of whom more later) tried to defuse this controversy with their song 'Can Blue Men Sing the Whites'.[6] The fact remains that black musicians' authenticity – or perceived authenticity – seems to excuse them from being discriminated against on the grounds of age.

6 Peter Cook and Dudley Moore and Monty Python also took the mick out of mindless adulation of black musicians. Peter Cooke asked Dud, portraying a coloured musician, 'exactly what colour he was'. The Pythons created a man called 'Blind Lemon Pie'.

Not so Groovy old rockers

For the past three months on my way into London on the tube I have passed massive blow-ups of photographs of the Rolling Stones, publicising their performance at the O2, formerly the Millennium Dome. Time hasn't been on their side. PR has. Keith in particular is certainly facially Groovy, but he seems to have been rebranded as some kind of fierce ancient tribesman you might meet in a high-end BBC2 documentary about anthropology. When Keith's autobiography comes out, it will no doubt have an excellent black music moment, and he himself seems to be trying to become a member of an entirely new one-man ethnic group in order to cope with the ravages of old age.

I haven't bid to interview any of the grand old men of rock 'n' roll. This is not because they'd say no. Although I did ask Brian May for an interview, but then saw a photograph and realised what he seems to have done to his eyebrow colour and withdrew the invitation. I wanted to talk to him about a return late in life to astrophysics, not Queen. Or The Queen.[7]

Old Rockers and other musicians, with rare and honoured exceptions, are exempt from these deliberations. As Steve's dad, when I finally tracked him down, put it on the phone, 'It's their business to stay young.' If they've managed to stay

---

[7] May, you will remember, stood atop Buckingham Palace and at the climax of the 2002 Jubilee celebrations played his guitar version of 'God Save The Queen'. Oh dear.

in the public eye or ear from the sixties or seventies until now, then they've almost certainly lived a life insulated from what the rest of us would call reality and are therefore either deeply Groovy or not at all, it's irrelevant. Like the celebrity Bad Boys, they're a bit like fictional characters.

This can all be illustrated by a tale of two Richards, Keith and Cliff, neither of whom, for opposite reasons, is in my gang. Cliff has withstood grooviness (facial and metaphorical) with admirable consistency and steadfastness. And Keith vice versa, with an emphasis on the vice. Neither belongs in the real world. Moreover, any musicians who attempt to 'make a comeback' using their hits of more than twenty years ago are, by definition, outta here, for obvious reasons, and this applies to The Monkees as much as it does to the Sex Pistols and Led Zeppelin. Enjoy the past, but don't recycle it cynically, would be the message.

That's not to say that groovy old rockers don't shape the thinking of Groovy Old Men, and Groovy Old Men in waiting. The fact that The Stones (average age 63) can still command an O2 audience, still function as a rock 'n' roll band, makes them inspirational, iconic even. It's tough for them to keep up the bad boys of rock thing, but they still give it a go, although sometimes it looks a bit forced. After their O2 show in 2007 they were publicly rebuked by Greenwich Council for ostentatiously smoking on stage. No wait, that's wrong. Greenwich rebuked them for the smoking. I'm rebuking them for the ostentation.

But it's tough being in the first wave of Groovy Old Men

– or Groovy Old Rockers. And I want to stress again that I think these are the first in a new wave of old men, and others will follow with greater ease. Perhaps controversially, I'm toying with the idea of admitting Jools Holland, when the time comes, to the GOM Hall of Fame. In a way, he's the James Last of his generation and therefore the last you'd expect to meet between these covers. On the other hand, Jools has always seemed to do what he likes, has caused us to re-evaluate Lulu and Tom Jones, he's at home with old jazz gits and young rock turks and still drinks in the south-east London pubs of his youth, although he now lives in a smart pad near to Buckingham Palace. It was at a Jools gig in Rochester Castle, the one at which I met Rico Rodriguez, that I had my second Groovy Old Man moment. Lulu (born 1948) was doing her set, and I watched a fat man in his 60s dancing raptly to 'Shout'. He was impressively nimble, with a hip-flicking move that incorporated a kind of torso aftershock.

Older people dancing is an important topic. 'Your dad dancing at a wedding' is now a common embarrassment scenario for a younger generation. This is because dancing (especially at a wedding) is a powerful metaphor for sex. But it's only comparatively recently that dancing to popular music became the prerogative of the young. For years everybody danced. And older people are reclaiming the dance, as they are reclaiming music. In China they ballroom dance on the street before work. A senior psychologist and academic I met proclaimed that the key to lasting happiness is Scottish Country Dancing (this may be taking things too far). And Spanish/Latin

American dance, especially salsa, is attracting an older generation. Instinctive, intuitive, un-ironic, improvised moving to music is one of the best indications of style. Which is why I did not have to interview this old fat guy. I knew, from two minutes of watching him dance, that he was as groovy as Rico. Back though, to better known potential rock-Groovy Old Men.

Here is my definitive list of rock 'n' roll Groovy old white men. Others like Keith Richards may be *icons* for GOMs, in the same way that Judy Garland is an icon for gay men. But the list in full is as follows:

Bob Dylan.

That's it, sorry. And Bob, you're lucky to be there because the rule here, strictly speaking, is No Americans. The reason is simple. In Britain it doesn't come easy. However, there are already plenty of useful cultural templates for American Groovy Old Men. Cowboys with weather-beaten faces. Ancient Native Americans. Ol' country stars. Woody Allen, Tony Bennett. They've had access to the universality of denim and great authentic music longer than we have. They've had more ageing movie star icons. American men are statistically less reserved than British ones. Not to mention the hats available, that can in many cases be worn without irony.

Every so often in the sixties, magazines and newspapers would do a feature along the lines of: 'The Swinging Blue Jeans/Herman's Hermits/Brian Poole and the Tremolos are the kids' pick of the pops … *nowadays*! But what will they all look like in 30 years' time … *when they draw their old age pension???!!* We asked the clever guys in the art department to "mock up" pics of your favourite beat heart-throbs to see what they'll look like when they're SIXTY-FIVE!!!' Brian Wilson of the Beach Boys actually looked forward to ageing a bit, mainly for sexual reasons ('Wouldn't It Be Nice' etc.) but only two songwriters foresaw the contradiction that time would effect on an entertainment profession divided by age-apartheid. Paul McCartney (no chance, Macca!) rather sweetly asked whether we would still need him or feed him. Well, feed him, yes. Royally. Need him – well, not so sure.

And, of course, Pete Townshend sang 'I hope I die before I get old'. Has he lived to regret it? I don't, by the way, want to hear that Townshend meant this 'metaphorically' and that this was a neat way of saying 'I hope I die before my attitudes fall victim to the culturally conditioned sclerotic effects of age, which in a future shaped by the liberalities of the sixties will mean old blokes can wear denim.' Oh no. It's a great, deliberately shocking line meant at the time it was coined, quite literally. The only way truly to stand by it would be to die on the brink of old age. In a way, murdering PT would be doing him a favour as well as creating eye-catching publicity for this book and for the already depleted Who.

A tempting scenario unfolds. I lure PT to a country where assisted suicide is legal. Or perhaps he's already there, taking the waters or having plastic surgery. I interview him, and confront him with his own very public suicide note. He stands by the line. With his testimony repeated on tape, I administer deadly poison or other humane mode of termination, photograph the body, then call (I haven't decided the order yet) an ambulance, the police, my agent and the *Melody Maker*.

Scenario two: Townshend recants. Rewrites the line as: 'I hope I live to a ripe old age.' Begs to be given a high GOM rating and a modelling contract for Paul Smith. I forgo the assisted suicide plan and accept second best. 'Who Man Changes Mind' isn't a bad headline. Not as good as 'Who Man Dies *Just* Before He Gets Old',[8] but never mind. So. Ring *Melody Maker*. Discover the *Melody Maker* is no more. Phone *Q* magazine.

Perhaps I won't interview PT at all. The whole plan seems flawed. Mind you, so does the line. And let's face it, he *did* want to cause a big s-s-s-sensation. He was born in the forties at a time when being middle-aged was the default setting for humanity and old age an acceptable consequence. He wrote the song when mutually agreed young/old apartheid was in full swing. Nobody to blame. It happened. Historical tensions created a deep f-f-f-fissure. But Townshend took it one stage further, suggesting that early death would be better than ageing. It belongs (albeit in less sinister form) alongside 'Arbeit Macht Frei', the Nazi death camp motto – a catchy slogan hiding something rather unpleasant. But now though, the age group who sangalonga Townshend, hoping to die before they got

8 And nowhere near as good as the similar line from the American humorous magazine *The Onion*: 'Commemorative Plate Industry Cries Out for the Tragic Death of Barbra Streisand'.

36

old, have actually started to *get* old. In fact a lot of them are old. But nowadays 'old' can mean something different to what it used to mean.

I should add, by the way, that not being a Groovy Old Man is perfectly OK. These guys aren't an elite, they're just a type. An interesting type, certainly, and one which will become more and more common, I hope. But there are plenty of perfectly pleasant men over 60 with predictable taste in music, a passion for car-cleanliness or azaleas, a subscription to the *Spectator* and no, no regrets. Their wedding-dancing may not be up to snuff, they may own some trousers with elasticated waists and … well, you get the picture. Please don't worry if the man/dad/granddad in your life fails utterly to be Groovy. In fact, forget I said 'fails'.

You wouldn't, by the way, find any GOMs among the cast of the Zimmers, a group of pensioners who in 2007 had a surprise minor hit with the Townshend song. Their perform-ance also benefited from ironic use of the lyrics, but their fame has all the hallmarks of a public relations stunt. According to the web-blurb, 90-year-old Alf, 'whose beloved bingo hall is being shut down', has, I think been hijacked. The Zimmers' website gushes that the performance, much viewed on YouTube alongside skateboarding ducks and sneezing pandas, 'exposes the disgraceful way we treat our old people in this country – and challenges a whole host of preconceptions about the elderly by taking them on a true rock 'n' roll journey'. It does no such thing. It's a mirror image of the sixties colour supplement stunt of ageing a then-youthful Mick Jagger, just for a laugh, to see what he looks like when he's 64. The Zimmers stunt put a bunch of pleasant-seeming, ungroovy and totally inno- cent oldies in metaphorical Beatles wigs, just for the humorous inappropriateness of it, and made them sing That Line.

I hope they enjoyed it, but some of them seem bewildered by the whole thing. Anyway, no Groovy Old Man would be seen dead looking like that. Or singing that. Would they, Pete?

CHAPTER TWO

History Men

'Things We Said Today'
Lennon and McCartney

I was going to start my chapter about the significance of Groovy Old Men's Recent History with: 'Every image of the past that is not recognised by the present as one of its own concerns threatens to disappear irretrievably.' But then I thought the Marxist critic and philosopher Walter Benjamin might be a bit heavy. So I went for the pithier: 'You can't escape your background.' Which is one of my mum's.[1] But Lennon and McCartney's romantic song in which lovers forward to a time when they'll remember important things from the past does the job. Groovy Old Men look forward, but have a fine sense of the past.

In 1947, Michael Foot defiantly argued that Britain's children at the time were 'healthier, tougher, stronger than any breed of children we have ever bred in this country before'.

1 Marxist, no. Critic, yes.

He omitted to go on to say: 'Now all that is needed as they grow older is a healthy dose of rhythmic Afro-American musical culture; an end to compulsory military service; a growing awareness of social change; technological, sexual and economic revolution; an increase in the number of crisp flavours available and a redefining of gender roles. I foresee, in the early 21st century, a breed of ageing British men, many of whom will still be sexually active; able to play the stock market and four chords on a guitar; change a nappy; take an interest in current cultures; work the newest machinery; cook, work, go out of an evening and be in control of their own hairstyles.' In 1947, of course, most Groovy Old Men were Groovy Young Teenagers, Groovy Little Boys or Groovy Little Babies. And 1947 is the cut-off year for the first elite generation of Groovy Old Men.

There is no upper age limit. There are some impressive early examples from the art world. David Hockney, born 1937. Peter Blake, born 1932. Call it the Picasso factor. Seeing things afresh for a living makes the living longer, perhaps. Certainly all the best specimens have refined cultural tastes, and a lot are creators in their own right. One of them, David Style, even invented a gizmo for slicing the bottom off doors without taking them off the hinges. The guy's no Michelangelo, but he changed life for the better for thousands of carpet fitters with just an idea.

No question that Groovy Old Men have journeyed along a marvellously diverse historical timeline. In the case of almost all of them, it's an appreciative awareness of that timeline that counts, even though their early years are shaped in a time of drab uniformity, post-war anti-climax, housing shortage and even hunger (Michael Foot was repudiating rumours of malnutrition among the post-war poor when he spoke about the healthy children of 1947). This is historian David Kynaston's view of Britain just after the war in his book *Austerity Britain*:

'A land of orderly queues, hat-doffing men walking on the outside, seats given up to the elderly, no swearing in front of women and children, censored books, censored films, censored plays, infinite repression of desires ... And despite women working wartime jobs, few quarrelling with the assumption that the two sexes were fundamentally different from each other. Children in the street ticked off by strangers, children at home rarely consulted, children stopping being children when they left school at 14 and got a job.'

Rationing. A housing crisis. Economic gloom. Hiroshima and Nagasaki. The shifting certainties that came with peace – sleepless strangers arriving home and wanting to be called daddy, mothers readjusting to housework after an exciting time at the munitions factory, relentless rationing – all this goes on while our guys are very little. They share the first whiff of freedom in the form of entertainment – of which there was no shortage whatsoever. Cinemas, dance halls, theatres, all full of empty-stomached patrons. Think *Annie Get Your Gun*, *Oklahoma*, and later Princess Margaret getting extra clothing rations for her wedding dress and nobody minding. The very fact that this torchbearing group of original Groovy Old Men arrive at a time of low wartime birth rate, before the boom, makes them all the more special. They're rare. Let's line them up, on the starting grid of 1945, these toddlers, titches and babies, a little later than the short-lived jollity of VE day. And I'm going to choose 29 July 1945, because on that morning came the first phenomenon to have a real effect on our heroes – even the tiniest of them – with the chimes of Big Ben followed by Sandy Macpherson at the theatre organ. The BBC Light Programme. For a generation, a guarantee of music and laughter wherever they went. The BBC consciously making light of the future, while the heavier-going, wholesome Home Service droned on elsewhere. Although it probably didn't sound that different to the BBC output that went before, it was promised by the BBC Director General Mr W.G. Haley (no relation) to be 'built for the civilian listener ... The BBC must not cease to innovate. Listeners will be tolerant towards experiment.'

There would be a lot of music, but it would be a while before Mr Haley's new network would rock around the clock. Nevertheless, this was for many tiny earholes an 'on all day' station, thanks largely to their mothers' choice. A lot of the content on that first day doesn't look that promising. Some dramas, the Torquay Municipal Orchestra's *Marriage of Figaro* and Violet Carson[2] fronting up the North Pier Orchestra in *Music from Blackpool*. It wasn't until 9.45 that we got the

---

2 As a sufferer of deliberate selective dyslexia, I always misread her as 'Violent Carson' and imagine a shadowy black-clad cowboy figure, prone to bouts of unreasonable nastiness even worse than those of Ena Sharples.

promising-sounding *Accent on Rhythm* with the Bachelor girls. Let's hope mum stays tuned, chaps, and keep your ears peeled.

Alan Coutts, born 1944 in Liverpool, remembers:

'I had some great times as a young 'un in the late forties and early fifties. One of my earliest memories was watching the Firework Display for the 1951 Festival of Britain. There was a crowd of us "on the Oller" next to Gerrard Crescent, overlooking Scotty Road and watching the display in the air over the Mersey. It was dark (I was seven years old) and I got separated from the family and managed to get back to the pub and sat on the steps waiting for me mam to come back. (When she did I gorra belting 'cos she had been looking for me for ages!!)

'I can well remember the Saturday morning Matinee at the "Gatey" (the Gaiety Picture House) in Scotty Road, watching films by that unforgettable group of cowboys, Tom Mix, Hopalong Cassidy, Roy Rogers and Gene Autry. Films also of the "Back Entry Diddlers", a group of urchins always into mischief. Much like ourselves really. There was also the inevitable "serial" every Saturday.

'I can recall saggin' from St Anne's School and getting a "Legger" on the Tate & Lyle Lorries going up Bevington Bush, slashin' the sacks with a penknife and nickin' handfuls of brown sugar off them.

'Making "bows and arrows" out of canes and in the hot summer "tippin' de arrers" with blobs of melted tar from bubbles in the road an' dippin it in cold water to harden. We would then shoot them into the air to see who could go the highest or who could go furthest across the "oller". We never ever pointed or fired off an "arrer" at anyone else!!!

'In late autumn, a great deal of time was spent after school collecting "bommy wood" from the "owl ouses" and the timber yard in Clairey! (Clare Street, back of Christian Street.) Goin' to the "bommy" on "Bommy night" on the "oller" near the pub, by the old Wash-house on Christian Street/Springfield Street (Springy Street).

'Beggin' "pennies for the Guy" from the people queuing outside the Odeon Cinema on London Road. Notice that the "Gaity" on Scotty Road was a Picture House but the "Odeon" was a Cinema!!!!

'Mayday processions come to mind when all the Catholic kids (I was a "proddy-dog"!) used to get really poshed up and march in procession to Mass to get "Confirmed". I can recall taking the pee out of a few of my Catholic mates when they had their faces scrubbed white and hair slicked down with Vaseline or lard!'

At the time of writing, I know nothing about Alan other than he's in his mid-60s and had a great childhood. But I can't help hoping, on the basis of this slim evidence, that he turns out to be a prime specimen. Because what we see in his account of being a Liverpool kid in the late forties is in stark and colourful contrast to the black-and-white drabness of the times. If anything, it wasn't the deprivations that made things so bad, it was the uniformity, the rules and regulations, the over-organising of everything.

For Terry Shepherd, born 1937, son of a bus conductor,

this conformism was a family as well as a social thing. Terry is now a prime early specimen who, in denim, black T-shirt and arty bling, could easily be in his 50s, not 70s. 'There was definitely an alienation between fathers and sons', he recalls, acutely. 'They were terrified that you would do something unacceptable.' His early life in the forties and fifties was to be entirely shaped by convention and the decisions of others: grammar school, apprenticeship, National Service.

Terry Shepherd was lucky enough to have witnessed a landmark live performance when he was five. In an aunty's parlour, his cousin Doris's GI boyfriend sat at the piano and played boogie-woogie. The 70-year-old Terry, ignoring the row made by the blokes now building his kitchen extension, looks back at the five-year-old and grins with glee about what he calls 'the defining moment in my musical taste'.

'I thought Christ, what's that? That's great! It sort of gelled. He was a white guy … I mean I still like listening to Pinetop Smith and Meade Lux Lewis. It was that sort of, you know, boogie. And it stayed with me. And when I heard it again years later, as a teenager, by trawling around listening to music, I thought "That's it!"'

The fact that Terry still likes boogie, the fact he has an insight into how that experience shaped him, his denim jacket and earrings, his collection of Dalí-inspired surrealist paintings (artist T. Shepherd), his guitars, the variety of his experience (apprentice, musician, soldier, layabout, trader, teacher), the clarity with which see sees his history, are all very pleasing. This is because Terry is Steve's dad, the bloke in the pub, the bloke at the gig, the man who I vainly tried to identify as a member of the mediastocracy, but who turns out to be an ordinary, or rather not so ordinary bloke. He is Groovy Old Man serial no. 0001. And retrospectively, he has a very clear vision of the discontinuity between his generation and the one before that made him what he is today. Even in matters of radio, then the biggest mass medium, he didn't see himself as part of the ITMA generation, more a Dick Barton fan.

However, even *Dick Barton, Special Agent* was a victim of the times. In 1948, concern about the violence and racy flavour of the radio series was voiced in Parliament. As a result, the BBC wrote a twelve-point rule book for Dick, including a limit on violence to 'clean socks on the jaw' (it went without saying that Dick wore clean socks on his feet, always black, to match the shoes); no sadism, even from the baddies; and a limit on horror effects 'such as night prowling gorillas and vampires', which were to be 'avoided'. And Barton was forbidden to drink, flirt or swear. Writing in the *Hollywood Quarterly* at the time, radio critic Dorotheen Ingham Allen saw this as typifying the difference between American and British radio. In America, such interference would be regarded as undemocratic. Here, it was par for the course.

All this desire to organise and regularise wasn't just a nanny state Labour government's work, or the result of a war during which obedience was a life and death matter. People were willingly rule-bound; they didn't see a contradiction in mass holiday camps being fashioned from military bases, they wore hats, smoked fags, queued quietly, dressed alike, foxtrotted round the dance halls in the same direction. Americanisation of any kind, in fashion, music or culture, was seen as something of an invasion for a generation with a residual resentment of American late entry into the war, and what was then referred to as 'Vulgarity'. An age in which, according to radical historian Raphael Samuel, 'a man who wore suede shoes was morally suspect'.

For David Style, then seventeen, and still stylish after all these years, 1947 was his summer of love, and I suspect there are those who would have called him 'morally suspect':

'In 1947 Brighton Pier opened and I started doing beach photography with my flatmate. All these people, pouring onto the pier, England had been so miserable you couldn't believe it. But that wonderful summer of 1947, I loved it, lots of girls. I was dressing in snap brim hat, sharp suits and shirts made to measure; I used to model myself on Humphrey Bogart. I still do in a way. With a bit of money in my pocket I was jack the lad, I had my own motorcar, a little pontoon boat …'

David's convinced that one word sealed his success as a beach photographer, and then as a nightclub photographer. 'You always asked couples or groups whether they'd like their picture taken *together*.' 'Together' was a big war word. British people had been determined to get through the war together, and the same spirit pertained when it came to the peace. And David, a teenager in 1947 rather than a boy as most of our

GOMs were, spotted it, albeit unconsciously. A new, pleasure-seeking togetherness. To say no to the picture was to reject a new society. So, this was a time of expectations, not all of them great, but a lot of them focused on these favoured boy children, who, if they played their cards right and rolled with the punches, rocked with the cavemen, would become the heroes of this book. And their first job was to break free of Austerity Britain.

If we accept the thesis that Groovy Old Men went through puberty at the same time Britain did, the dates that fix the timeline involve the arrival of live rock 'n' roll, the departure of compulsory service in the armed forces and the onset of puberty. The first two of these can be pinpointed with some accuracy. The third's a bit hit and miss. The rule of thumb dictates the two fixable dates as 7 February 1957 – when Bill Haley and the Comets arrive in the UK and Tommy Steele does a week at the Chiswick Empire – and February 1959, when the end of National Service is announced. If we put the onset of puberty rather arbitrarily at fourteen, then we might have the little chap born in February 1943, with a fourteenth birthday on the very day that Haley plays the Dominion in London. Too young to be among the 3,000 at the Dominion show, he hears a rare airplay of the song on the BBC and imagines it dedicated to him. Groovy Old Men's musical history – in a way more important than any other influence – can be scrutinised more carefully in the next chapter.

Two years after Bill Haley's visit he gets an even better

birthday present. At sixteen, he hears defence minister Duncan Sandys'[3] announcement that National Service, hitherto more or less compulsory for the over-eighteens, would come to an end. Our hero quietly sighs with relief. He'll be the first of a generation of young men in nearly a century not to have the prospect of fighting in a war as part of his future. The last intake of National Service personnel leaves Civvy Street in November 1960. Three months before his eighteenth birthday.

3 Arguably, Duncan Sandys has an extra significance in this history, not just because he ushered out conscription, but because of a rare and exciting gadget in his possession at the time he was planning the end of National Service. In a celebrated divorce case involving the Duke and Duchess of Argyll, Sandys was revealed as a possible paramour of the Duchess (who, it was claimed, became a nymphomaniac as a direct result of a fall on the way back from the chiropodist). The divorce case took place perilously close to the Profumo affair, giving the then Conservative government an extra helping of the willies. The evidence is a 1957 photograph of the Duchess, naked but for pearls, giving a blow job to a man who can't be identified, as his head is cropped from the picture. Sandys was at the time 49, so too old to be a GOM of any kind. The GOM connection – and the proof of identity – is in the nature of the camera, not the photograph, nor the activity. Was the headless man Sandys? At the time nothing was proved. But he was eventually nailed by the Duchess herself, who deliberately revealed much later that at the time the picture was taken, the only camera of its type in Britain was in the possession of the Ministry of Defence, hinting that Sandys must have brought it with him to liven up the proceedings. So, nothing groovy about a cabinet minister having illicit sex with a toffess, but you may think ownership of Britain's first Polaroid camera worthy of the front cover of *Stuff* magazine. And a feature of Groovy old manhood will be his taste for, well, things.

Rock 'n' roll historians might insist we adjust the dates forwards. Born 1941, young fellow-me-lad gets to pubesce to Bill Haley's earlier 'Shake, Rattle and Roll', which reaches number four in the UK chart in 1954. He's keen-eared enough to quiz his father on the lyrics, 'I'm like a one-eyed cat, peepin' in a sea-food store', and clip-round-the-eared enough not to persist. He too gets wind of the end of conscription (hearing about it in news of the Defence White paper in 1957). But he's eighteen in 1959, one of the reluctant rump of squaddies who didn't have a choice. So he's called up.

Whether they got caught in the National Service net or not, the fact that they knew it was ending is the clincher. None of my GOMs talked about King and Country, duty, the value of a military background. Here's John Peel, born 1939, demobbed 1959, on his experience:

'I can be immensely boring on the subject of national service. As virtually no one I know served, I can tell them almost anything and although they may suspect I'm making it up, they can't really know. I hint darkly at working on secret projects I dare not discuss and excuse myself from physical activity by patting my leg in a sort of resigned way and saying "Shrapnel. Korean War. Don't like to talk about it." No one ever says "Hold on, you were only twelve when the Korean War ended, you twat." Although they could.'

Peel (writing there in the foreword to Trevor Royle's book *National Service: The Best Years of Their Lives*) was among the last of 14 million British men to be called up in the 20th century, 2.3 million of them called up between 1945 and 1963, when the last pressed squaddie finally got his freedom. Since 1916, teenage males had taken it more or less for granted that fighting a war, or training to fight a war, was going to be part of their future. It's hard for later generations to imagine that ever-present danger. But after the shambles of Suez, the modernising of conventional post-war weapons, the explosion of the first British nuclear device, and the realisation that men in khaki would not be able to protect the UK from a nuclear attack, the idea of a standing army ceased to be valid, politically, militarily and personally. War wounds, or the idea of them, were becoming a self-deprecating joke. Hence John Peel's lightheartedness about Korea. As soon as the expectation of fighting was over, National Service began to mean something different.

According to Trevor Royle, 'Because an obligation to military service had existed in Britain since 1939, few families had not been affected by the nation's flirtation with its armed forces. Fathers and sons had a common bond in their military service, military terminology and slang were acceptable within the family, and the armed forces were not the closed societies they were to become. But by the later 1950s the times were changing. In the first ten or so years after the war, society had changed little and the immense effort required to put Britain back on its feet bred a rough kind of solidarity. Those same fathers and sons united by their National Service also shared the same dress, appearance and tastes.'

But it was a bond that ended at the end of National Service. A new kind of man emerged. For the men in khaki with no war to fight, there was an absurdity to those last years. Corporal Iain Colquhoun remembers:

'Demob was almost unreal, like being in a trance. The military train took me (only passenger) to Liss, thence by BR to Haslemere, Waterloo and home to Scotland. I stopped at London, saw a film, *The Blackboard Jungle* with its opening music of "Rock Around the Clock". Much as I hate rock music, I still like that one and I still have a 78 record of it.'

Those who didn't endure the 'trance' of emerging from National Service might have had a tinge of disappointment about missing the whole experience. In 1957 Peter Kay, born 1943, was a Yorkshire teenager with a passion for motorbikes and things mechanical. He had mixed feelings about narrowly missing call-up. He was 'partly disappointed at missing the chance to muck about in tanks'. He was free to carry on his studies at agricultural college, where he realised he was really interested in motor engineering. Today, in his mid-60s, he still runs a one-man haulage business in Northallerton, has country and western on the truck stereo and still rides a motorbike, as he has done almost all his life. Whether National Service would have tamed him, made him less of an individual or more of a mechanic, is impossible to tell. But retrospectively, he says 'Thank God I missed it.'

'The older boys who went off for their two years came back men', says Ian Gardhouse, born 1945, with a tinge of envy. 'Society treated you in a different way if you'd done it. You had something approaching the status of someone coming back from the war.' For the officer class this meant greater acceptance in the establishment. For the non-officer class it was more likely to mean far less.

Recent oral histories about National Service feature almost exclusively those who are unanimous about its positive effects. Most come from the officer class. They talk of short sharp shocks, responsibility, standards, masculinity. Laurence Bell, interviewed in Tom Hickman's book *The Call Up*, reflected that 99 per cent of those conscripted turned up when called up. Bell thinks if National Service came back now the no-show rate would be 50 per cent. The end of conscription was a turning point. 'Today society is ruled by sentiment and emotion. As a nation we've gone soft and the sexes have moved closer together. National Service was a very masculine thing and the general run of chap took it in his stride and National Service tightened him up.'

The opposite way of looking at it would be that since 1914 society had to be ruled by discipline and order for the sake of military strength. When the need for that subsided, we could be more honest about how we felt. The sexes enjoyed moving closer together. Being a good soldier involved a very tight and restrictive kind of masculinity. When it all ended, men started to loosen up. Thank goodness.

A number of men I interviewed talked about the potential for travel, improvement, education, that the armed forces might have brought them but didn't. Terry Shepherd did serve and ended up thinking it had been a waste of time. He'd wanted to go to Hong Kong, but ended up in Germany, learning, blind to the implications, to parachute into the east

– 'enemy territory'. But it wasn't adventure that Terry had on his mind. It was money. Parachutists got paid more.

David Style, fine figure of a GOM, strategically 'got belly-ache'. He seemed strangely reticent about how he dodged the call-up, as if some authority could 40 years later 'do' him for it. But at the same time, he stresses it was easy to dodge. 'Why would I want to do that?' he asks, as if National Service was optional. Ray Gosling did the same thing. Dodged it. And strangely, discussion of dodging it seemed to touch a nerve. Our conversation, verbatim:

RAY: But I managed by some careful chicanery, is that the word? Chicanery? Is it when you dodge and dive or whatever it's called, I managed to get out of the National Service.

NB: How?

RAY: It's none of your business.

NB: Well of course it's my business.

RAY: Well it's your business to ask the questions but I'm not bloody telling you how I managed to get out of it …

NB: Why did you not want to do it?

RAY: I don't think anyone wanted to do it.

NB: Why did you not want to do it?

RAY: What, who wants to do two years in the bloody army being ordered about when you've got rock 'n' roll in your hearts?

Royston Ellis, who enjoyed one of the grooviest fifties and early sixties of all, put it in a nutshell and then in an email to me:

'There was a freedom in the 1950s that our elder brothers

and parents never had because of the 1939–45 war. I was too young by a few months to be caught up in National Service so escaped that unpleasant conformity.'

Very few of the men I talked to at length regretted missing a chance to serve King and Country. At worst it was a waste of time, at best its function was that of a kind of 'finishing school', in which fun and social mixing was the prime outcome, not toughening up or battle readiness. Professor Laurie Taylor got called briefly into the RAF, and was promptly expelled for medical reasons. He suspects the armed forces didn't want a potentially sick passenger on its hands. He has happy memories, having been demobbed, of relaxing with servicemen pals at SHAPE – Supreme Headquarters[4] Allied Powers Europe – in Paris, where the facilities were excellent and nobody seemed to question civilian guests. The whole post-National Service atmosphere was summed up by the hit ITV sitcom *The Army Game*, in which a standard issue Sergeant Major fumes with rage at the increasing impertinence and incompetence of his squaddies.

Andrew Kerr, a terrific example of a Groovy Old Man, was born 1933 into an upper-class family with sturdy roots in the establishment. The family, traceable back to the Duke of Wellington, had strong associations with the Royal Navy and the Conservative Party. Andrew was naturally seen as officer material through and through, except that by the time he did National Service he was already learning to live with a

4 Motto: *Vigilia Pretium Libertatis* – The Price of Freedom is Vigilance.

misleading label he wouldn't fully understand until he was much older. The misleading label read 'stupid'. In fact, it was Kerr's 'stupidity', later diagnosed as severe dyslexia, that was the cause of his grooviness, more so than his collision with rock 'n' roll or his experience in the Navy. That, and how he dealt with being 'stupid', makes him unusual. Had Kerr been conventionally able academically, his life story might have followed a more conventional path. As it was, he was subject to routine cruelty at public school. He suffered regular beating for academic failure, wasn't allowed home to see his mother after his father's death because he had been 'gated'; and he left without distinction. His home life wasn't that much better. With little affection on offer and the lasting effects of school leaking into life in the school holidays, Kerr accidentally called his mother 'sir' on more than one occasion.

He was deemed too 'stupid' to be an officer. He didn't mind, but the Navy did. It wouldn't do to have someone who spoke with an officer's accent in a below decks uniform. But despite its best efforts, the Navy couldn't square Kerr's class and 'stupidity'. Kerr, on the other hand, found this easy. As a steward, he found instant popularity as the 'bubbly bosun' dispensing the daily tot of rum with generous abandon and enjoying the leftovers with gusto. Below decks, he found no problem fitting in with members of the lower orders and had a great time. 'As long as you're not snooty, it's fine', he remembers. And he ended up as a stores assistant, never going to sea. The fact that this is at the end of National Service and Kerr didn't have to face danger or see action is significant.

From Andrew's voice on the phone, I'd expected to meet an eccentric old hippy. A Viv Stanshall kind of guy – Edwardian velvet 'n' satin smoking jacket, attention-seeking facial hair, little tasselled hat, possibly. Loveable eccentric old hippy. Wrong. Meeting Kerr in his neat little west country house – surprisingly free of stuffed bears or Indian hangings – and hearing his life story, another criterion for being a GOM emerges. That of being a nice guy. If, after all the discussion of historical factors, that seems a bit limp, I suppose I'd have to default to an argument about nature and nurture. Kerr's life story is amazing, personally and in the grander historical context, but the shaping factor for him isn't suddenly being hit by Haley or missing active service. It's a kind and positive openness, the ability to face adversity head-on, and not getting twisted, numbed or normalised by it. Groovy Old Men are born as well as made. And they've got to be likeable.

It's possible to flip the logic and identify a man with all the shaping factors needed: no serious National Service, early exposure to youth culture, a minor part in youth culture history, a creative and enterprising nature, a love of poetry. Felix Dennis – entrepreneur, publisher, former crackhead and hero of the sixties counterculture – has all these attributes, yet from meeting the media manifestation of the man, I don't think he'll qualify. If I'm not careful, though, the definition of a Groovy Old Man will just be 'an old man I like' and that's not good enough. So history has to play a part.

* * * * *

It's pretty clear that a classic generation of GOM is born in the early- to mid-forties, into a newly demilitarised time zone, in which music played an increasingly important part. Some are born earlier than this and, despite being well into their 70s, are impressively Groovy. So, no upper age limits. I'm declaring an arbitrary lower age limit, though. Men born after 1947 don't count as members of the first wave.

That doesn't mean those born after won't become Groovy Old Men. Many more certainly will be. But these older Groovy Old Men are the pioneers, the first of a kind, the originals. The next wave won't have that cachet. David Hepworth, for example, writer and broadcaster and publisher of grown-up rock magazine *The Word*, starts ad sales presentations saying proudly: 'I was born in 1950 and that gives me the winning ticket in the lottery of life.'

He then goes on to chart various landmarks he has in common with his generation. He was just aware of Elvis before he went into the army in 1957.[5] He was thirteen when The Beatles broke. He was fifteen when he heard Bob Dylan sing 'Like a Rolling Stone', seventeen when he bought his first Hendrix record. These landmarks mean his generation are of an age to buy cars, cameras and mobile phones that he hopes his ad-business audience will advertise in *The Word*. At 57, his age when we met, Hepworth, aka the Rocking Vicar (his

5 It's a widely held rock truth that Elvis was ruined by service in the army, and that his best period was before 1957. Fits nicely with the theory that military service does nothing for male style.

online persona, a tellingly jokey reference to older establishment-type men), is one of the most erudite and knowledgeable people in the music press. But I have to urge him to look again at the numbers on his lottery ticket. He's three years too young to be counted a winner. He's a youthful aspirant, a deserving runner-up.

At seven, he might have been dimly aware of pre-draft Elvis, but to get the full force you had to understand what the bloke was doing from the waist down, and preferably to realise that this was a white man doing stuff usually associated with black men. By the time The Beatles broke, Elvis had swapped his khaki for a commercially attractive Hawaiian shirt and the money men had established commanding positions on the beach-head of youth culture. To be a member of that elite cadre leading the offensive, a first-hand sense of change is crucial. The birth boom that peaked in the later forties and early fifties resulted in sixties teenagers (including, I have to say, me), none of whom looked back over their shoulders and saw war, the threat of war or the danger of having to be trained to fight, or austerity and hunger. These men can't remember a time before rock 'n' roll. The classic specimens, born in the early- to mid-forties, experience the end of war culture and the start of teen culture. The real winning lottery ticket is issued in 1940. Winners are sixteen when rock comes to the UK, and seventeen when they hear they ain't going to study war no more.

Education – more by default than design – played a huge part in our boys' shaping, if not in their liberation. Despite

Labour's victory, the chance to create an egalitarian system went unseized. In fact, it went more or less un-mulled over, despite the reports and White Papers on education ground out during the war that toyed with making education fair. The only genuine reform was free school milk. For our purposes, the continued system of educational apartheid – private education, grammar schools and, for the majority, secondary moderns – provided some useful texture in the growing medium. Eleven-plus failures and those labelled 'stupid' are over-represented in the ranks of Groovy Old Men. The envies, resentments, rejections and other useful side-effects of this apartheid ground in them the first of their grooves. Gave them 'outsider' status. I'm not endorsing this as a benefit of apartheid, because for most children of both sexes it helped spell monotony.

Sartorial rule-breaking was becoming a fact of life. For Terry, a long-lasting fact. He passed the eleven-plus, prompting a familiar mixture of joy and angst in his parents. Pleased he was clever, worried about the cost of the uniform. At his grammar school he soon noticed a bizarre fashion phenom-enon in his elders but not betters. The drape blazer. This garment was a history lesson in itself. Perfect (but probably not prefect) daywear for the period. With its coat of arms and its special shade of maroon or blue, it combined traditional public-school values – slavishly aped by the grammar schools – with a glance back at the long-coated Arthur English 'spiv' character and a glance forward at the rock 'n' roll uniform of the new Teddy Boy. But this garment was for those who could *afford* to combine school rules and fashion, and Terry's form of style-protest was to wear the same blazer for as long as he could – till it was a shrinking wreck. Ditto the compulsory school cap, which almost disappeared into scandalously long curls. The power of suede shoes to offend paled in comparison.

It wouldn't be long before men singing about blue suede shoes would rock the world of the growing boy, who for the early fifties had been diverted by new jet aircraft, land speed records, the Goons and the first IBM electronic brain being plugged in to do active service at a factory rather than a research laboratory. There was also another blue fabric that, in the mid-fifties, might have caught his interest. The number one fashion item was denim jeans. For women. Although the Rosie the Riveter female war garb wardrobe had been rejected in preference for more 'feminine' styles, appearances by Natalie Wood and Audrey Hepburn in denim inspired a generation of young women to wear jeans. The messages sent to little boys' unconscious minds must have been baffling. 'Why is my mummy/sister/auntie dressing like a cowboy/train driver/factory hand? More to the point, when do I get a pair?'

The denim timeline is almost as important here as the GOM one. For years, denim was seen as indivisible from youth, rebellion and America. The ultimate in informality and the first genuinely unisex clothes item. Later, in its 'designer' phase, it became desirable, expensive, middle-class and eventually middle-aged. Men and women in their 40s in the eighties agonised about wearing denim until 'designer' denim made it OK. But there was still an undeclared age limit. Your dad wearing denim could still be as bad as him dancing at a wedding. Over the last twenty years that limit has eroded and denim is being recognised as perfect for the oldest generation as well as everyone else: cheap, hardwearing, soup-resistant, lots of pockets, easy care. And Groovy Old Men (and okay, women) have led the way. It's no coincidence that wrinkled country star Willie Nelson is a poster boy for GAP.

For Terry, in retrospect at least, the grammar school experience meant very little. Although he left with ten O-levels, the chief significance it had in his life was still the cost of the uniform. The school leaving age was fifteen, and he stayed till sixteen. Another cost. As everything changed around him (except possibly his family), he was learning to be a dissenter, to question everything. And, in common with a lot of Groovy Old Men-to-be, he was learning that he wasn't a joiner. No organisation for him. He doesn't think it would have made any difference had the 'unilateral' educational ideal – later to be called the comprehensive – been put into place after the war. The only benefit he saw at the time was that grammar school introduced him to middle-class kids whose tastes in music reconnected him to his cousin Doris's boyfriend's boogie-woogie. Kids who could afford to indulge their musical tastes with pre-rock 'n' roll American records, still hens-teeth rare at a time when the BBC had only just ended a ban on dance music on Sundays. For Terry and others, American Forces Network Radio became required listening. As music is a key factor in GOM's life, there's a chapter devoted to it.

After school, Terry and his ten O-levels – without much guidance or choice – went into an apprenticeship at EMI. Not the record division, sadly, but the electronics one, where he learned very little and watched his National Service date loom nearer and nearer.

I've promised to ring-fence music for another chapter. But part of Terry Shepherd's history is important here. In his mid-teens, Terry had managed to get a guitar and started, with the help of a Bert Weedon instruction manual and his mates, to play skiffle and folk blues, and was going in for contests and playing minor gigs. On 'the circuit' he was bumping into not-yet stars like Marty Wilde and members of what would become the Rolling Stones. Then came National Service, and by the time he was free of it, the musical opportunities that he remembers wistfully as being 'wide open' in 1957 had gone. Taken by the privileged kids whose student credentials had kept them out of the forces.

'That's why possibly most of the people who got into music after that period when I came out, whatever, from then on, were probably middle-class', he observes. 'I mean the guys that I'd been in the band with, a couple of them had married and were into mortgages and stuff like that. I mean I was just rattling around really, I mean just screwing anything you could and making enough money to get by on.'

But if young middle-class student types were filling the musical gaps left by Terry and co., who'd gone off and done square-bashing, there were other avenues that were becoming 'wide open' in the late fifties. At that time, no professional foot-baller could earn more than the maximum wage, calculated to be on a par with skilled artisans. But a young Jimmy Hill, a Brentford player and chairman of the Professional Footballers' Association, started a controversial campaign to allow players to earn unlimited pay. Making it (eventually) as attractive to aspire to be the new Tom Finney as it was to become the new Tommy Steele. To paraphrase a young denim-clad Marlon Brando, anyone could now be a 'contender'. A working-class hero *was* something to be. In this respect, two later gurus from diametrically opposite ends of the political spectrum were right. John Lennon and Keith Joseph. Sure, Lennon meant it ironically: 'There's room at the top they are telling you still,/But first you must learn how to smile as you kill.' Joseph, meanwhile, though he was the brains behind the Tories' new agenda for classlessness, revealed a deep distaste for the lower orders.[6]

No reason why our Groovy Old Man shouldn't have benefited from both viewpoints. Part of the art of becoming one is the ability to adapt to the times. But if a Groovy Old Man is something to be, I can't help wondering whether it could ever be possible for a decidedly *non*-working-class hero, someone more Group Captain Peter Townsend[7] and less 'I

6 His accusation that teenage girls were deliberately getting pregnant so they could jump the housing queue meant that he was out and Thatcher was in.

7 Yes I know he's far too old, but former royal equerry Group Captain Peter Wooldridge Townsend, CVO, DSO, DFC and Bar did break down some social barriers by shagging Princess Margaret in the full glare of the media spotlight. At around the same time Duncan Sandys was more quietly fiddling with his Polaroid camera.

was born with a plastic spoon in my mouth' Pete Townshend, to become a Groovy Old Man.

Initially I had my doubts. I was to be proved wrong, again and again. Andrew Kerr, who we've met already, was certainly born with a silver spoon in his mouth. Now, after a diverse career both inside the establishment and way outside it, he is by his own account 'a bit skint'. But totally Groovy.

Another source of teenage tension that marked Groovy Old Man's teenage years was the Cold War. And born out of the Cold War came a mass-killing weapon that might have impressed a teenage boy, despite elements of it being shrouded in secrecy. A weapon of which the Russians were secretly jealous.[8] James Bond, undeniably top-drawer in origin, was stylish to the point of vanity, instantly attractive to women in a way that left Kenneth More and David Niven types sucking impotently at their pipes. He was overtly self-indulgent, vain and ruthless in matters of sex, hence the secrecy, mainly on the part of dads, who bought it saying that James Bond was a modern James Hannay, then hid it to stop others getting at the naughty bits. And the character, already a champion of what would be Groovy Old Values, begat a GOM icon in the

---

[8] According to 'private information', Peter Hennessey confides in his excellent book on the fifties *Having it So Good*, Bond movies 'became much sought after by the KGB in Moscow and that even allowing for filmic exaggeration, a degree of envy about the gadgetry and women at Bond's disposal aroused a degree of envy about the lifestyles of their western counterparts'.

shape of former milkman, Sean Connery.[9] If it seems perverse to feature Bond before Bomb in the influences on the growing Groovy Old Man, my defence is that this was a reflection of government and media at the time. Also because the eternally young Bond will surface later in this book.

Using 21st-century rearview vision, we want our 1950s teenage GOM to have been instantly outraged by the nuclear threat. One simple reason this didn't happen was because people didn't know much about it. According to the 1955 Strath Report on the effects of nuclear war on the UK, a successful Soviet night attack on main population centres using ten hydrogen bombs, each containing a 10-megaton nuclear warhead, would kill 12 million people and seriously injure or disable 4 million others.

'This would mean a loss of nearly one-third of the population. Blast and heat would be the dominant hazard, accounting for more than 9 million fatal casualties, against less than 3 million from radiation. Four of the 16 million casualties would be caused by a single bomb on London.'

Enough, you'd think, to have teenagers reaching for their duffel coats and taking instantly to the streets. But the Strath Report was kept strategically secret till 2002. The fifties

9 During his time as a milkman, Connery's round included Fettes School, where James Bond was educated after getting chucked out of Eton. Fettes's other star pupil – T. Blair. Despite the Strat and the jeans, Tony will fail to become a GOM, although his influence in the GOM community will be widespread.

establishment was just as worried about the threat posed by the invasion of American comics – occasioned by paper shortages for the awfully wholesome children's newspapers from before the war – and questions were asked in Parliament, but there was less that could be done with that. The earliest manifestations of the Cold War were carefully controlled, mythologised even, in a way that meant our teenage boys, if they took any notice at all, seemed to place it in the past. If they did get radicalised, it happened later in the sixties, and probably the late sixties and a more distant war. The first significant post-war male military icon isn't the Bomb, it's the Bond. Handsome, well dressed, vain, self-seeking, rebellious, promiscuous and as renewable as Dr Who. And a patriot to boot!

It's tempting to imagine a 'what if' scenario in which the explosive properties of pelvis-grinding rock 'n' roll and detailed knowledge of the effects of bone-powdering megadeath weapons (developed with our Groovy Young Man's apprenticeship tax-pound) coincided. And while we're playing Time Lord, let's pre-date the Pill by eight years, just for fun. The results are excellent, if a little frightening. The danger might have been that our young lads would have been too busy shagging to be interested in Bill Haley *or* to protest against the Bomb.

However, there was a general feeling in the fifties of not wanting to look back – airbrushing out Nagasaki and Hiroshima, and among the generation in which I'm interested, treating the seemingly minor conflicts in the Middle East and Korea as the folly of the war generation. Arguably, the Labour Party could have created a radicalised group of young people with an impassioned argument for unilateral disarmament in the late fifties. Instead, shadow foreign secretary Aneurin Bevan did the opposite. He made an impassioned speech at the Labour Party Conference in 1957 for multilateralism – which many at the time and now see as tantamount to being pro-nuclear weapons. The original CND badge – later an emblem of pride among the young generation – belongs on the tweedy lapel of a slightly older generation whose idols were Bertrand Russell and A.J.P. Taylor. It's worth remembering that this is a time when only a tiny minority went to university and the voting age was 21. Few in the current GOM line-up would join CND in its first manifestation.

However, Groovy Old Men are linked, in a way, to Grumpy Old Men, who in turn owe their existence to the invention of Angry Young Men, who surface at this time that the GOM generation are growing up. Angry Young Men (a phrase coined by interesting but non-Groovy J.B. Priestley) were quintessential tweedsters.[10] They experienced early tremors of the qualities we seek, but the difference is in the music, or lack of it. Angry Young Men, untarnished by rock 'n' roll (or, for that matter, for the most part, sex), didn't turn into Groovy Old Men. Angry Young Man prototype Jimmy Porter in John Osborne's *Look Back in Anger* is significantly a trad jazz fan,

---

10 A tweedster is a man who thought differently to his dad, but dressed the same.

and he's deeply influenced by the death of his father who fought in the Spanish civil war. But he's too bitter to become Groovy, and collapses in the end. His creator John Osborne was also far from Groovy. Kingsley Amis was counted – wrongly, probably – as an Angry Young Man, but it's *Martin* A. who might eventually be a Groovy Old Man, a member of the second wave. Despite his hair, and his politics. However intertwined (history and politics, not hair and politics), we must leave the question of whether Groovy Old Men have to stay true to their radical roots – and whether radical roots are necessary – to a later chapter.

Few tweedsters morphed into Groovy Old Men. Many were well-informed enough to be early CND badge-wearers, and for that we should give them all credit, but their Afro-American music of choice was trad jazz, which perhaps unfairly was and still is seen as deeply ungroovy and swept away by rock before it could get started.[11] All the same, that first wave of CND badge-wearing late-fifties/early-sixties rebels did produce the first important wave of rebellion needed for GOMhood. A few of them also enacted one of the first demonstrations of how much they cared about their music and how much they derided other people's.

They did this by having a fight. Which will break out halfway through the next chapter.

---

11 A distorted vestige survived in the shape of *The Black and White Minstrel Show*, whose cheerful racism survived till 1978.

CHAPTER THREE

Rock 'n' Roll

*And the devil drives 'till the hearse arrives, you lay
that pistol down.*

Ian Dury, 'Sweet Gene Vincent'

I'm on the phone to David Style. I want to see if he's got a music moment. He wants to go to the Bonzo Dog Doo-Dah Band gig. With eighteen Glastonburies under his belt, he's a live music man. He first saw his favourites, the Super Furry Animals, when he was in Japan with his son, at the Fuji Festival, a couple of years back. 'I downloaded a couple of tracks but I didn't like them. But when I saw them live I changed my mind.' And he's still crazy about The Beach Boys. That was his music moment, The Beach Boys at Glastonbury 2005. Although it could just as easily have been jiving at the Hammersmith Palais in 1948. Except he can't remember any of the names of the bands. He may be a Groovy Old Man but he's still capable of 'senior moments'. So he'll plump for The Beach Boys at Glastonbury.

'I don't go any more. Glastonbury. It's too poncey. Too commercialised. They lay too many rules on Eavis nowadays.

I liked it when it was rough …' My question about his tastes resurfaces. 'And Fado, I like. Reminds me of the Portuguese connection.' Oddly enough there's another Fado fan coming along soon. In the 1970s, Style was involved in an interesting though slightly dodgy adventure in Portugal. I can imagine it, a mini movie, a clever geezer in the antiques trade versus some anonymously uniformed men, all set to a soundtrack of Portuguese soul. But I steer him back to his music moment. How blokes like him have lived through half a century of changing soundtrack. 'You're not the first to observe that', he says, drily. 'Anyway, I'm not what you call a great collector. I haven't got a huge load of CDs.'

He listens on the radio, in the silver Audi, late at night. 'Coming home from gigs, maybe. I went to one in the West End the other night with a pal, well not a gig exactly, a kind of 20s night. Had a few drinks, danced with a few girls, a bit of a laugh. Wore two-tone shoes, black shirt, white tie …' I interrupt him with lines from the song 'Sweet Gene Vincent'. The Ian Dury reference isn't lost on David. Nor for that matter is the Gene Vincent one.

But Style wears his long music education lightly, and can be as enthusiastic about Soft Machine and early Pink Floyd as anything new he might hear on *Late Junction* on Radio 3. He's also a big silence fan. And he's not the only one. Nowadays, he depends on the radio more than any other source. And though his sensibility is highly tuned, he is no musical anorak. 'Why should I make any differentiation? If it's good, it's good.' He agrees with me that there are plenty of blokes of his generation similarly conditioned to enjoy music. He sees them at gigs. The recent Brian Wilson gig at the Albert Hall. Glastonbury's full of them. 'Old hippies?' 'Freaks, we used to call them.' Hippy was a term of abuse. How does he feel when he reads about music in the press and it's all kids, in tribes he's never heard of? Does he feel excluded, airbrushed out of a picture traditionally rooted in youth?

'I don't care, either way', he says, economically. 'Fuck 'em.'

* * * * *

In the same week, Mike Bell, the man who's installing an iPod on his ride-on mower, is in paroxysms. Transports of wheezy laughter and delight. He sits on the pale green sofa in the dinky hotel suite above Portobello Gold, the pub he's run for 25 years, and thrashes at the cushion, breathless with joy at the memory, his face turning as crimson as his corduroy shirt. The year is 1965. He's 20-something, in America, with green card, so he's dodging the draft as well as ducking and diving in the second-hand car trade (this is the bloke who still has a 52 Buick as a souvenir of those days), and he's hooked up for some reason with his hero, country and western fingerpicking star Chet Atkins. No mean guitar player himself, Bell's in the back of Chet's pickup one day, picking out the latest Beatles tune, 'I Feel Fine'. The solo.

'Mind if I pull up and you show me that lick?'[1] drawls Mike, imitating Chet.

---

1 You can hear what might conceivably be the result on 'Chet Atkins Picks on the Beatles' – RCA 1965. Track One.

'So there we are in the middle of Texas and *I'm showing Chet Atkins how to play guitar.*' Thump, wheeze, laugh. This is Mike's happiest story, he's unabashedly ecstatic at it. More so than the time he got a ride in a jet plane when he was a teenager, more so than any memories of either wife, or the time Bill Clinton dropped in to the Gold for a beer with 25 heavies and a helicopter escort.

Music moments are intensely important for Groovy Old Men. The early ones stick. Terry Shepherd, conditioned as an impressionable five-year-old by exposure to live boogie-woogie at his aunty Doris's, was rocketed back to that moment the first time he heard rock 'n' roll. The year was 1954, when 'Shake, Rattle and Roll' was released in the UK, but Terry thinks the records that got played at the west London youth club he frequented were imported from America by someone's dad in the know. The reaction, according to Terry, was unanimous: 'Fucking hell, what was that?' The impact was, in today's terms, incalculable. Only a very select few in Britain – Terry among them – had heard rock 'n' roll's predecessors. Terry had, thanks to mates at grammar school, heard the wailing R&B saxophone of Earl Bostic on American Forces Network Radio. One of his mates' dads was American, and he knew what to listen out for. The 'pre-rock 'n' roll' music of people like Louis Prima wasn't that widely known except to a lucky few who'd heard the skiffle tracks included on Chris Barber's Jazz Band and Ken Colyer's Jazzmen LPs. That's why Haley was such a shock. Because he was largely unprecedented. And people of Terry's generation had a chance to be in at the start.

In the austerity years of the late forties and early fifties, the music most people came across was on the wireless, in the dance hall, or, if they were very lucky, on the home gramophone. The experience, by and large, was a passive one. Music was 'provided' in one way or another, by the BBC, by the dance band, by the music publisher, by the piano teacher. It was rationed and distributed by a higher power. In wartime this was conscious propaganda, music designed as a morale-booster for the masses. The idea that any ordinary person might spontaneously make their own music for mass consumption by singing and playing was outlandish. The very few exceptions like Gracie Fields and George Formby became idols, partly because of their ordinariness. And at the same time they became instant establishment figures. But for most, up until the mid-fifties the potency of cheap music was experienced passively.

Noël Coward has a lot in common with Ian Dury. Both Groovy Old Men of their time.[2] That near-cliché, 'extraordinary how potent cheap music is', from Coward's *Private Lives*, is still as valid as its replacement cliché: 'sex and drugs and rock 'n' roll' – both freeze-dried explanations of the power of pop. The potency is sexual (in the play it's the trigger for the divorced Amanda and Elyot to revive the sexual part of their

2 It's not known whether Coward knew Dury's work. But in 'There Ain't Half Been Some Clever Bastards', Dury wrote: 'Noël Coward was a charmer/As a writer he was brahma' (which is slang for 'an attractive girlfriend' or just 'good').

otherwise doomed marriage). Its cheapness refers to the 'nasty insistent little tune' playing in the background, which is Coward's own hit 'Some Day I'll Find You' – equally insistent, fairly cheap but redeemingly popular tunes went on to receive a thousand airplays on British wireless. A tune whose potency Amanda can conveniently blame for what she is about to receive offstage. But the era in which only very clever establishment figures like Coward could be in charge of that kind of music was coming to an end. Cheap music and sex – paired by both Coward and Dury – were getting together to form a revolt.

The potency of cheap music wasn't lost on journalist Ray Gosling, for example, deeply affected as a young teenager in mid-fifties Northampton by doo wop, which is linked inextricably in his memory with the first time he came into contact with real black people, as well as black voices coming out of a tuppenny jukebox.

'We'd never seen black people before. And they were unbelievably glamorous … unbelievably attractive, the Americans. And the jukeboxes had just come in and the music was enormously, enormously important. And I used to think it was me just on my own and then when I went back recently and talked to a Teddy Boys' reunion I found that we all felt it … We felt something in the music and it was black music. It was before rock 'n' roll, this was the Platters you're talking about.'

Ray, an enthusiastic doo wop fan and accomplished underage drinker in the pre-Haley 1950s, used to 'move' the black servicemen into the pubs where the jukeboxes played better music. This meant risking the apartheid that existed among American servicemen, because the pubs with the better music were the pubs colonised by the white GIs, who would try to ban blacks, so Ray's mission was egalitarian as well as musical:

'This was long before there were many blacks in England at all, but we were aware that the segregation was wrong. You've got no idea now about how deeply we felt about these enormous human issues that we didn't know as human issues until then.'

'Sh'boom' by The Chords had also entered the UK charts in 1954. Doo wop – street corner vocal music, sung in a private slang,[3] extemporised by black youths in Philadelphia and Manhattan, heavily influenced by be-bop jazz but sweetened by the romantic pop of the day – had one distinguishing feature that made it attractive. It wasn't cheap music. It was free music. Music people made by themselves, made to be sung in public. This was nothing like the complicated dance band music on the BBC or the music hall-inspired round-the-piano family sing-song. Doo wop, early rhythm and blues, as well as blues of the kind played by Big Bill Broonzy, who toured Britain as early as 1952, was music that seemed stunningly accessible and liberating to Ray Gosling.

'The music was important but the other thing that was important was the fact that we suddenly developed a sense of colour, I don't mean black/white race colour. It was the

---

3 I wouldn't be the first to draw parallels between doo wop and hip-hop.

colour that you had in your velvet collar, the colour that you had in your shirt, the colour that you had in your lemon green socks, on your brothel creeper shoes; it was suddenly men had ceased to be able to be forced into being men. And men could suddenly explore their feminine side and that was the sort of thing that happened with the Teddy Boy era. And it was to do with the falsetto as well.' 'Only Yooooo!' he shrills, loud enough to be heard in the lounge of the sheltered flats where we'd had the Elvis conversation.

'Blacks were doing this. Black men were doing this. American black men were doing this and we felt that we could have luminous green socks and we did, and I'm not talking about London or Liverpool, I'm not talking about major places, I'm talking about ordinary little small towns in middle England, and there was this feeling of enormous freedom.'

Ray recently went back to his home town of Northampton in search of men of the era, and discovered the old old Teds of his teenage years, still true to that life-changing era. It reminds me of David Style in black-and-white and of 'Sweet Gene Vincent': 'There's one in every town/And the devil drives 'till the hearse arrives,/You lay that pistol down.' Some, like skiffle player Terry Shepherd, recognised that they too might be able to make music modelled on the authentic examples this chosen few had heard for the first time. Picking up the pistol, as it were. It was saxophone that Terry went for first:

'My whole ambition was to save up enough money to go to a shop in Wembley and buy an alto sax. It was always sitting in there. In fact, it was something you'd never buy if you knew anything about it. It was made of white, a white, what must have been an early plastic or something like that, with all gold bits on, but it looked the real dog's bollocks.'

The sax thing was abandoned. Guitars became the thing, not yet because of rock 'n' roll, but because Terry and a few friends had been turned on to American Folk Blues, then enjoying a bit of interest in early fifties Britain. At first, aged fifteen, they tried to make a guitar, then finally and belatedly, Terry managed to acquire one. Before long they were busking cinema queues in the West End of London. What they were playing looked like skiffle and sounded like it, but nobody had yet given it that name. Pete Frame's book, *The Restless Generation: How Rock Music Changed the Face of 1950s Britain*, tells how skiffle was nearly called 'spasm' music, and features a thorough and handy chronology of fifties rock in the UK. What emerges is the productiveness of the fifties scene, the enterprising nature of the musicians and the short-sightedness of the music business, the music press and the BBC.

I hope it's no coincidence that a number of my subjects did decide, many of them before pop's full-on commercialisation, to do it themselves, either as players, singers, or writers. Alan Coutts remembers being inspired by the simplicity of skiffle to try it himself: 'So much so that I remember getting hold of an old Oxo tin about 12" square, a thin plank of wood and some copper wire and made my first "guitar". I also made a "bass" out of a tea chest, brush pole and string, my younger brothers would play these instruments whilst my elder sister "kazooed" the latest melody through a comb covered with tissue paper!'

It was in this atmosphere of optimistic musical DIY, round the corner from Alan Coutts in Liverpool, that John Lennon and Paul McCartney famously met for the first time at a garden fete in Woolton, in 1957. John already had a band, the Quarrymen, and Paul, on the basis of good looks and superior guitar technique, was invited to join. At that time the idea that this was a way to make money was only just dawning. The music was the important thing.

So, in a movement that came out of trad jazz, some British teenagers had started a music revolution. They'd seized the potency of cheap music and made it their own. This had happened in parallel with rock 'n' roll, which came pre-packaged and ready-Americanised. Ray Gosling, who makes no bones of the fact that he dodged conscription, thinks the end of National Service pales into insignificance in comparison with the beginning of rock 'n' roll:

'National Service was always something that you could duck and dive out of and people did. But, you have to understand this, it's really important that you understand this, rock 'n' roll was as big an event as the Protestant Reformation. It completely overthrew the world in the way that [the end of] National Service never did or never could do.'

Ray's enthusiasm for his theory is infectious. Who, experiencing such a colourful revolution, with such diverse after-effects, could *fail* to be a Groovy Old Man 50 years later? The answer, sadly, is 'a lot of people', and here, maybe, those who say the concept of GOM is all about wishful thinking have a point.

The DIY atmosphere persisted and Ray found himself part of it. Just about to drop out from Leicester University (ten years ahead of the time when dropping out became cool), he tuned in to – or more accurately bumped into – a rock 'n' roll band that played because it liked playing, more than for the pin money it brought in. Ray's real ambitions were towards writing. His flirtation with the music business is told in full in his autobiographical work *Sum Total*. It's his skills as a journalist that get the band noticed. He writes a successful press release headed 'Beat group can't get a look in', but it's his idealism that propels him towards management, the ideal of a music event run by the kids for the kids, with Ray taking any profit that might accrue.

Then (as now) Ray had a repertoire of jobs, and he set off to raise some money to get the band a venue by working on the railway. This done, Chez Ray's opening night – 'the only dance in town run for the lads by the lads' – was counted a great success, with attendance around 100. 'I was business manager, originator, ideas man, stage manager, ticket puncher, manager, financial backer, the whole shoot rolled into one.' Sadly, Chez Ray made a loss, and continued to do so. Then Ray tried talent contests, again financed by his hard work doing casual labour and fuelled by his idealism. This is from an original handout of the time:

'The people who run it, those who sing and the boys in the band are all living in Leicester. You the people of Leicester are being offered the best that you yourselves can do. As often as we can we will run a club and a Dance like the Oh Boy session we ran at the Co Op Hall. If you think you can sing or strum a guitar or play a piano or anything like that you've only to let us know …

'It's your show we're asking you to support. It's your people we're asking you to dance to and dance with or just to listen or watch. The more of you who come, the more of you who perform, the bigger all this will become. If it flops it will be your fault.'

Again, the events were counted a success, but ran at a loss. Despite national press attention and plenty of memorable nights' entertainment, Ray found himself torn apart by the pressures of commercialism, idealism and what would later be described as 'youth work'. The bands and the halls hired wanted him to make money and keep order. Ray wanted to stick to the ideal of entertainment by the kids for the kids. A London-based charitable institution, nameless in his book, which had started backing the 'club', saw it as a way of 'civilising' troublemaking teenagers attracted by the music. Ray, himself a lad given to the image of lime green socks and doing cartwheels in the cinema during *Blackboard Jungle* without removing the fag from his mouth, didn't see the distinction between troublemaking and other clientele. He may have been an activist, and still is, but he wasn't a 'do-gooder'. And still isn't. This, and financial problems associated with loss-making gigs, led to him packing in his career as man-behind-the-music, still counting it as a success rather than a failure.

He'd made an impact. And rock 'n' roll, made for the love of it, had made a lasting impact on him.

Mike Bell's musical moment hits the time-target smack in the middle. It was 'Rock Around the Clock' on record, 1956, played very loud, and he heard it while walking across his school field, from 50 yards away; the first thing he heard was the bass and drums, and found himself 'captivated'. Although I suspect he was just as captivated by the fact that he was hearing music sufficiently amplified to be heard from 50 yards.

'The point was that it was loud and my friend had on a Wharfedale loudspeaker in a concrete drainpipe. That's all you could do. And that's what it was, it sat in a concrete drain-pipe, the sound. It was a good sound.'

Mike Bell was fascinated by the technology as well as the tunes. His friend across the field introduced him to the joy of audio: 'I remember his name, Peter Angelo, and he had made the very first hi-fi system that I think I'd ever heard, from a kit. He built a Mullard 510 or something. It was 5 watts, you know. And then he built a Mullard 10, something which was 10 watts per channel and then …' This doesn't mean he's a nerd. It means that on the days when he gets to the pub he runs so successfully, the first thing Mike does is adjust the sound system. He cared then and he cares now. The kids he has working for him don't understand graphic equalisers. He does. Back in the fifties, Mike's DIY tendencies went beyond the knob-twiddling and the soldering iron. At first his ambitions were boogie-woogie-wards. Piano. Two things diverted him. One was a rockabilly sensibility, picked up from Bill Haley. The other was the piano stylings of another soon-to-be radio star,[4] a star whose tinkling shone so bright that it put Mike right off. 'I'll never be that good', he thought. So he decided to make it on guitar. And he decided to make his own guitar. And then he taught himself finger-style guitar, then he taught it to other people, then he went to the United States and taught Chet Atkins a Beatles lick or two, then came back and worked for the massively successful Gerry Anderson TV puppet empire, as an assistant director on *Captain Scarlet*, hired for his technical and artistic 'can do' abilities, all the while indulging his passion for hi-fi by creating what he regards as the first street-bothering in-car system.[5]

Who, experiencing such a colourful history as Mike's, Ray's or Terry's, could *fail* to be a Groovy Old Man 50 years later? was a rhetorical question that turns out to be testable. By pure coincidence, within days of asking, I stumble across the means to answer the question: *The Big Beat Scene* (2/6, illustrated), 'an outspoken exposé of the teenage world of rock 'n' roll', published in the same year as Ray Gosling's *Sum Total*, operating in a lot of the same territory musically, and written by Royston Ellis, born in 1941, then 'one of the most outspoken teenagers in Britain'. Whereas Ray's book is impressionistic and personal, Royston Ellis's book is written in the style of

---

4 It was, of course, Vincent Duggleby, later to become star of personal finance shows *Money Box* and *Money Box Live* on BBC Radio 4, neither shows known for having barrelhouse blues tendencies.

5 12-inch Wharfedales, reel to reel and vinyl record players, in a Mini.

popular journalism. Would one of the most outspoken teenagers in Britain turn out to be one of the Grooviest, most Outspoken Old Men, some 46 years later?

Ellis's cover image bears a startling resemblance to a Steve Coogan creation (as does some of the book's prose, but he did write this at eighteen, over 40 years ago, so let's not be too harsh). And, at the age of eighteen, according to the blurb, he gatecrashed Radio Luxembourg.

'Since then he has appeared many times on Radio and TV. A Poet of some repute, he wears a beard through family tradition. He is also a Duke of the Caribbean island of Redonda.' As the first line in a GOM CV, you couldn't get better.

Most of *The Big Beat Scene* is a straight biographical account of the stars of the time – Bill Haley, Adam Faith, The Shadows (with whom Ellis proudly performs some of his poetry on TV). But Ellis starts the book with a colourful and detailed account of the life of a semi-professional rock 'n' roll band, Tavy Tender and his Teensters, and their one-night-stand at a dance hall in Buckinghamshire. On weekdays they have workaday jobs. But the weekends are different.

'There is Johnny, a long-legged, sleepy-eyed guitarist, whose lithe young body weaves and twists onstage as though possessed by gods of primitive African tribes. The bass player, Twink, is a bouncing boy with a shock of red hair crowning his chubby face. The clown of the team and a gifted mimic, he is a character the Teensters fans adore … Mick is the drummer, a short young fellow, naturally quiet until he is sitting behind a set of drums. Then all his shyness vanishes as he "beats the skins" and thumps out a rhythm for the boys. "It's a swinging town", says Tavy. "*That's* where the chicks are.'"

Ellis seems to have hit tabloid pay dirt here, because Phil, the Teensters' manager, 'has had the distinction of being exposed as a teenage drug addict. Admittedly the "drug" was only the strips inside a nose inhaler. The story goes that Phil, as soon as he learned that there was a journalist enquiring about his favourite drug, bought up supplies as fast as he could.' Phil's savvy stunt pays off. He buys as much inhaler as he can find and when the story's published, he makes a profit.

The evening goes according to plan. Fags smoked, power sockets abused, amplifiers cranked, and ears duly split by the volume. Beehives are back-combed, skirts twirled, shirts stick to heaving chests. Girls who might turn out to be 'lays' sought. A drink spilt, a punch thrown among the gyrating bodies. This being the sticks, the fashions are a bit behind, with the occasional drape suit in evidence (probably squaddies from the unfashionable north who've been out of touch for a while). The sequence culminates next morning in tagalong local girls Hazel and Babs, groupies in all but name because the name hadn't been invented yet, being unceremoniously dumped and left to hitch home by Johnny and the boys. They've got to do it all again that 1960 Sunday night, and there's no time to waste on niceties. Bliss was it in that dawn etc.

But what of the teen journalist and observer Royston Ellis? Should we feel as used as poor Hazel and Babs to discover that 'Tavy and the Teensters are an imaginary group, though they are typical of the spare time popsters who are an essential part of the big beat scene'? Did he make the whole thing up? Or is it an accumulated account of dozens of nights spent in the company of Phils and Tavys and Hazels and Babses? And if there's an element of journalistic licence here, is it unfair to confront him with this 46 years later? But wait, the young Royston has shown some terrific forethought. 'The era of sneering at young people enjoying themselves has finished. Gradually the big Beat has seeped through to the oldsters who find that they too appreciate the lively sound and gay rhythm.'

If my theory that Groovy Old Men are the result of early and significant exposure to youth culture, especially musical youth culture, is true, then Ellis must be found and questioned. It's one thing for me to talk to men who are already demonstrating strong GOM counts, and conveniently concluding that their current style is connected to their teenage experience. But what about reversing that perspective? Ellis is a teenage specimen preserved in paperback in 1961, accurately predicting that pop would end the generation gap before it properly began. Now that he's an oldster himself, what's the effect of the seeping of 40 years of 'lively sound and gay rhythm' into the system? If Royston Ellis can be found and assessed, there's an even more powerful proof of the theory that Groovy Old Men are significantly conditioned by music from their youth. So where is Royston Ellis? How does he dress, where does he live, what's on his iPod?

From a brief trawl of the internet, more amazing Royston-related material emerges. Ellis was a beat poet who performed at Liverpool University and met John Lennon in 1960. Lennon is quoted in the hippy paper *The International Times* saying that Royston introduced The Beatles (pre-Ringo) to drugs, or rather the insides of benzedrine-based inhalers, as used by the semi-fictional Tavy and his Teensters, and very possibly Hazel and Babs. Before the Mighty Quinn, before Doctor Robert, he might have been the first A-list drug dealer. So where is Royston Ellis? There are, rest assured, more sex 'n' drugs and potent cheap music revelations to come.

Tavy and his Teensters weren't the only musical revolutionaries. In Ellis's book he makes it clear that it wasn't just rock 'n' roll that made an impact. Before mods and rockers fought on the south coast, in fact before mods had been invented, two other tribes went to war, a war about jazz. It culminated in the Battle of Beaulieu, on August Bank Holiday 1960, a significant event in GOM history, referred to in Royston Ellis's book as 'a complete fiasco'. David Redfern, who can't help being a Groovy Old Man, having been a music photographer from that day to this,[6] took pictures of the fight, and gratifyingly much of it was broadcast on television.

'It erupted when the TV cameras went live', Redfern told *The Guardian*. 'Suddenly they were up in a lighting gantry, bottles were flying and they were advancing onto the stage. There were probably only about 200 or 300 but it was getting nasty!' Battle lines were drawn between supporters of trad

6 His pictures can be seen on the web, but they also adorn Mike Bell's Portobello Gold, shortly to be renamed the Portobello GOM.

and bebop, the traditional jazz fans loyal to the authentic sounds of New Orleans, and the bebop beatniks arguing for the merits of Charlie Parker and modernism. Beards and sandals, tweeds and turn-ups versus berets, black polo necks and duffel coats (worn with ironic deference to the dying militarism of the age). The traditionalists might claim the moral high ground with their claims for authenticity, and their CND badges. And trad jazz was by far the most popular, with hits like 'Petite Fleur' and 'Strangers on the Shore' riding high in the early sixties charts. The modernists – who allegedly started it with a controversially beboppy set by Vic Ash and Harry Klein – claimed to represent the future of music, and the future of beards (goatee versus full, enjoying a revival in the nineties). Acker Bilk, stripey-waistcoated tradster, played an especially long set to soothe the festival goers, and later claimed even more controversially that the beatnik hooligans weren't real beatniks.

When Popular Culture becomes an examination subject at A-level, students will be asked to explain the significance of the Battle of Beaulieu, 1960, in terms of (1) Music; (2) Politics; (3) Fashion; (4) Groovy Old Men; and (5) Social Class.

This is the model answer:

(1) **Music.** The battle was an early demonstration of the potency of music, particularly live music, whose young listeners were fuelled with the powerful narcotic of cider, in a bucolic setting especially commissioned for the purpose. Music not only separated the young from the old in this

way. It also demonstrated that young people, especially young men, were prepared to have a fight with each other about it, such was their diverse passion. See later mods and rockers etc. The rift – followed by minor violence – wasn't just the fault of the young. The media fanned the flames.[7] There was also a powerful musical lesson to be learned by police. One officer at a modern music festival is probably not enough.

(2) **Politics.** If the two-year-old Campaign for Nuclear Disarmament had had an Alastair Campbell or Tim Bell figure to advise them on PR, it would not have chosen to align itself with the trad jazz tendency. The image of Bertrand Russell, then aged 80-something, marching as to anti-war with a traditional jazz band, would have done little to attract the young, or to link music, modernity and activism in their minds. Groovy Old Men hadn't been thought of. Groovy Young Men weren't interested. (Ray Gosling thinks that, if asked, a lot of his Northampton Ted contemporaries would have been pro-nuclear weapons. But who'd have asked them?) Not CND's fault, of course, but it was, arguably, a trick missed, not to find a better beat to march to. Some have argued that the ungrooviness of trad is linked with its very 'traditionality' – going back

---

7 In his report of the battle in *The Guardian*, Stuart Nicholson quotes two headlines from *The Times* that year – 'Jazz Fan Charged With Burglary', and 'Jazz Fan Charged With Murder' – prompting *Jazz Monthly* to complain that it had 'yet to see "Butterfly Fancier Charged With Larceny", or "Stamp Collector Charged With Rape"'.

to comfortable pre-war, pre-social change music. Veteran journalist and defiantly ungroovy Alistair Cook was among the first to have a passion for it, which he discovered before the war. The 'nigger minstrel' image of *The Black and White Minstrel Show* was a comfortable watered-down version of trad culture which cheesily played to audiences of as many as 18 million, oblivious of its power to offend. It lasted 21 years. And Thatcherite minister Kenneth Clarke, a late-model tweedster, managed to present a programme focusing on authentic jazz on Radio 4 without apparent contradiction. Because there wasn't any. The relationship between popular music and activism has always proved to be problematic, with pop and politics enthusiastically but sordidly 'using' each other, then springing out of bed in a tiff when it all goes wrong.[8]

(3) **Fashion.** It would be wrong to say that the sartorial distinctions seen at the Battle of Beaulieu were completely along tribal lines. There were some who wore bear skins, for example, and not all modernists had goatee beards or berets. The sandals and bigger beards of the tradsters would reappear a mere seven years later in the summer of love. In reality the trad/bebop clash just added to the prêt-a-porter fashion show, from which, for most youngsters, pick and mix was the order of the era. There's a picture of Terry

8 See The Beatles invited to Number 10 by Harold Wilson; Oasis invited to Number 10 by Blair; ministers of the Crown choosing tracks by the Arctic Monkeys on *Desert Island Discs*, etc.

Shepherd with a duffel coat and a Tony Curtis-style haircut. Tony Curtis would never have been seen dead in a duffel coat. Meanwhile, a duffel-coated naval Kenneth More, as seen in *Sink the Bismarck*, pipe clamped between teeth, gazing out to sea, would have looked silly with a Tony Curtis haircut, on or off screen. Yet Terry Shepherd carried the combo off with the same aplomb he now confers on his denims and jewellery.

(4) **Groovy Old Men.** The Battle of Beaulieu helped form a perfect growing medium for the young GOM, who would go on to be bombarded by the fashion, social movements, tribal violence, politics and music of the changing times, and perfectly at liberty to pick and choose. (The fact that neither trad jazz nor modern jazz had much of a future in the charts, and both were to become rarefied tastes in Britain, is all part of the fun.)

(5) **Social Class.** Pop and politics may have had a troubled history. However, posh and pop have always got along fine. The spoon in the mouth can be plastic or silver, Pete. Wrong again.[9] A working-class hero is something to be. But a ruling-class hero can change things with the flick of a cheque book. The Beaulieu Festival was started by Baron Edward John Barrington Douglas Scott Montagu in 1956. Motto: 'a combination of blue blood and the blues'. It's a combination that's got on fine ever since, with many of the

9 Although the simplified line 'I was born with a spoon in my mouth' lacks impact.

rockastocracy and the Debretts mob sharing the same taste in Rolls-Royces and class-A drugs, both tribes having a fascination with the other. Traditionally, a wealthy aristo – or one with a crumbling stately pad and dwindling tea room income – decides to put on a festival. See Knebworth, Woburn et al. Andrew Kerr, born 1933, solidly Groovy, and escapee from the ruling class, honoured this tradition by helping to start the Glastonbury Festival, which he billed as the world's biggest midsummer party.

Kerr is more of a history man than a music man. He and his history between leaving the Navy and 1968 can be encountered later. His contribution to the British music scene is incontrovertibly huge. Without him there would be no Glastonbury Festival.[10] And although, as we've seen from his adventures in the Navy, he was always an outsider, he came late to grooviness.

Let's meet him in 1968, the proud wearer of a pink corduroy suit, the proud tenant of a flat in Groovy Notting Hill, the proud user of a lot of drugs, a man acquainted with the Churchill family, Jimi Hendrix, John Profumo and the Grateful Dead. By this time, outsider status is pretty 'in', and at a lunch organised by socialite aristo Lady Diana Cooper, Andrew

---

10 And, arguably, less opportunity for older artists to connect with audiences as part of the 'greying' of pop music. Just as politicians have always claimed to be Arctic Monkeys fans, old rockers started to flock to Glasto to get cred with alternative music fans.

finds himself monopolised by a fascinated Princess Margaret. Andrew, we have to say, was rather a beautiful young man. When I put this to him he agrees, modestly, and says this got him in a lot of trouble.

By the time Andrew is chatting to Princess Margaret, he's also bumping into lots of musicians and models, attending parties, doing lots of drugs. Jonathan Aitken invites him to join the new Yorkshire Television, where he meets Tariq Ali. A bit later he's helped by Ronan O'Rahilly, landlocked after Radio Caroline is banned, to start writing a book called *Heaven is a Planet*, showing how events outlined in the Bible might have origins in outer space. Drugs play a part. I did say this was the sixties, didn't I?

In 1970, with the sixties unofficially still going on, Andrew, now a reporter for the *London Evening Standard*, attends the Isle of Wight Festival, and disgusted by the commercialism he encounters, decides to organise a free festival. With his increasing interest in ley lines and natural energies, he feels Glastonbury is the ideal place to combine spirituality and music. Farmer Michael Eavis has already attempted a festival in his village of Pilton in 1970, featuring Mark Bolan who arrived in a velvet-covered Buick, and an ox roast that, according to some, was stolen wholesale by the Hells Angels on security. Luckily that was the only thing they got away with. They did not get away with murder.

Andrew co-finances, with what was left of his inheritance, the vegetarian 1971 Glastonbury Fair, as seen in Julien Temple's documentary about the whole Glastonbury phenomenon.

His partner in the enterprise is Arabella Churchill, daughter of Randolph, with whom he becomes firm friends. The line-up, for a free festival, was impressive and included David Bowie, Traffic and Fairport Convention. And if the 'dead hand of commercialism', as Andrew put it, meant that the Grateful Dead ungratefully didn't play, never mind. Here, fifteen minutes into the movie, is a young Andrew, a chunkily handsome soulful-eyed Jesus figure with a cross that once hung round his grandmother's neck. ('Oh I've still got that, I must get it fixed', he tells me.) Back in 1971 he told the world: 'We can't tell what good will come out of it till we try it.' The good that came of it can be seen in the bits of archive in the Julien Temple movie. Outraged locals confronting incoming fans; the worrying practice of 'festival'-style dancing, sometimes naked, always body-painted; and a concerned John Craven, in lapels wide enough to accommodate a fourth London airport, with an earnest report about the 'controversial' nature of the event. If the good from it is now mainly experienced by mobile phone marketing departments and BBC digital channels, never mind. Kick-starting the Glastonbury Festival, albeit with establishment cash, and being true to the 37-year-old freak you were when you're 75, makes you Groovy indeed. Lord Beaulieu concentrated on motor cars after the jazz festival ended. Andrew Kerr, from the same social bracket but a man for all seasons[11] with a distinguished and diverse CV, did a lot of other stuff.

11 Especially autumn, when he can indulge his love of composting.

Andrew Kerr came late to grooviness. Took his time. He may have possessed a pink corduroy suit in the sixties, but he didn't wear lime green socks in the fifties, nor did he cartwheel in the cinema aisles. He was too old for that. In this sense he was a late developer. So, in two ways, was David Style. In the fifties and sixties, Style lived in black-and-white. He continued his career as a photographer, taking black-and-white photographs, first in Ley On's Chinese restaurant, the first in Soho, then in nightclubs, where he spent most of his time in evening dress. He was a cool guy, no question, but he hadn't been struck by rock 'n' roll.

As a nightclub photographer, the trick was the fast turnaround, asking, as always, whether the punters would like their photographs taken 'together' and promising them a very quick memento of their night out. So he worked late, developing. Late developer,[12] geddit? Eventually he found a woman called Eileen to do his late developing for him, and developed an ultra-fast system of processing that guaranteed happy punters in the Embassy Club and elsewhere. They'd get their pictures the same night. By the mid-sixties he had gigs with fourteen nightclubs and eight pretty girls in little black numbers taking the pictures. Style never taught them photographic technique. He put little white marks on the camera controls: one for 'two-shot', one for 'crowd'. He denies keeping the girls under-trained so they'd just work for him. They were 'quick,

12 OK, it's a crap pun. But it will serve as a reminder that you don't HAVE to have started with Bill Haley to qualify as a Groovy Old Man.

bright' girls, but their brightness was to do with selling the service, not adjusting for the right exposure.

Style's soundtrack was nightclub stuff. Jazz, torch-song, nothing too hairy. But the great sixties nightclub aroma of Brut, cigars and money was soon to be wafted away by the then Labour government, who abolished a loophole allowing entertainment to be considered exempt from tax. Not before David Style, by then a father in his mid-30s living in Dolphin Square, had made a pretty profit. And not before he'd seen – and heard – the future. By this time he was a fully paid-up member of the Establishment, no pun intended. I mean Peter Cook's satire Establishment, where you could see Lenny Bruce or hear Dudley Moore. Style was (and still is) a sharp-looking guy. A sophisticate. Around that time, with the writing on the wall for the nightclub industry, Style started to diversify. By now an accomplished photographer, he offered his service to *The International Times*. His first gig was to photograph fifties heart-throb crooner Johnny Ray, and the resulting photomontage, turned into a triptych by Style, went down well with the hippies who ran the mag. Though why they should want pictures of a fifties heart-throb defeats me. David can't remember. But by this time, the great smell of patchouli, dope and macrobiotic catering had taken over. David went to the new psychedelic club in Tottenham Court Road, UFO, and heard Pink Floyd. Soft Machine. Dylan. Velvet Underground. That was it. For a while he was a part-time freak. For a while he'd leave the nightclubs in dinner jacket and cigar and show up at UFO, ready for a floral shirt and a joint. In the end he sold the photography business and opened a boutique in Brighton, where he'd been brought up and taken photographs on the pier.

Both Andrew and David are older GOMs and late developers. Which means that although they lived through the fifties rock 'n' roll era and remember it, they didn't join the revolution until comparatively late in life, as mature men. Once they did join, in the sixties rather than the fifties, there was no stopping them. Oddly, the familiar figure of the frozen-in-time Ted, Sweet Gene Vincent, doesn't automatically qualify. Seventy-year-old Teds look great, they're interesting and there's nothing wrong with them. Maybe remaining true to your roots is a key GOM characteristic, but maybe mummified Teds are too true. Time stood still for them when Elvis was drafted. Groovy Old Men adapt or die. Or, sadly but more accurately, they adapt then die.

So maybe it's time to adapt the theory. Rule 1, Groovy Old Men are older than baby boomers, stays intact. Many had formative experiences in the early years of youth culture. Some – but not all – had these experiences at youth culture's very birth in the mid-fifties. Others were too busy and joined in with the baby boomers. But if the answer to the question 'Do you remember when rock was young?' is 'Sorry Elton, I don't', it doesn't matter. If you joined in late, that's fine.

Another opportunity to experiment with the theory that music maketh Groovy Old Men emerges as I await a response to my enquiries, via his agent, about Royston Ellis, who should remember very well when rock was young. The opportunity is Social Networking. Saga, purveyors of insurance to the over-50 careful driver, launches Saga Zone (Facebook and MySpace for over-50s) at just the right time. Thirteen thousand men and women have already signed up even before the official launch, the oldest 87 years old. After the launch, and the familiar 'silver surfer' headlines, the population doubles overnight. At first glance, especially when you winnow out the women, this looks a lot like Victor Meldrew.com. But behind the discussion topics about gardening and whether it's OK to smack children (and I was sadly diverted, I have to say, by some enthusiastic child-beaters), there were plenty of music fans. The Saga publicity includes some familiar data about the increasing power of the grey pound, including the fact that 63 per cent have bought music online.

Plenty of Saga men like pop – and everything's mentioned, from Johnny Cash to Snow Patrol. An almost all-male debate about the greatest guitarist ever features plenty of 60-somethings arguing over Clapton, B.B. King, Al Di Meola, Django Reinhardt, Roy Buchanan, Rory Gallagher. A groundswell of 'Zoners' agree that music forums be more prominently featured on the site. Lots of profiles, men's and women's, proudly include diverse tastes in music. There's very little of the anti-pop prejudice that characterised older generations of over-50s. And there's plenty of evidence that children and grandchildren influence taste. A great place to look for Groovy Old Men and ask them about music. However, Saga forbade me to canvass directly. I couldn't just go online and write 'I'm writing a book about …'. Instead they wanted me to adopt the softly softly (or sneaky sneaky) approach. I needed to start a thread of debate based on some kind of provocation.

I enlisted the aid of a nice lady called Annabel Louise, depicted pictorially online as a bowl of fruit. I try various versions of my controversial opening out on Annabel, who scorns them as too pompous, too journalistic, too long-winded. In the end I post:

Has Music Kept Us Young?

We're the first generation to have enjoyed a pop music sound-track throughout our lives. Does this make us a new kind of older person? One with maybe a younger outlook? A 77-year-old mate of mine adores the Super Furry Animals and Aretha. I'm not saying we are all like this, or even that we should be. But how much does music – and I mean pop music – play a part?

Gratifyingly, someone posts:

I think you're partly right. I look at my generation and see a big divide between those, like me, who embraced the sixties (including its music) and still keep up with modern culture and ideas and there are those who didn't. Sometimes I come across people of around my age who could be my grandparents for the ideas and interests they express. I'm not criticising you under-stand they're just not like me and mine.

It turns out to be a 58-year-old legal secretary. Female. And although there's lots of talk about new bands and new old people, it's all from women. Initially the only man I get appears to be a Scot wearing a kilt with his legs open who says he prefers forties swing. Men like to list and argue. Their favourite forums involve hard facts and lots of dates, references to their 'collections'. And a lot of them seem to get stuck in genres they liked when they were aged 30–40 and stick there. It begins to look desperate. As many as 13,000 potential GOMs and I'm stuck looking up the kilt of a Glenn Miller fan.

'Surely it's not about keeping up with modern trends, but the memories of our past which our old favourites evoke, the girlfriend or motorbike of that time, the dancehall, the feelings, etc. etc.', says a 62-year-old bloke in the security industry.

'Of course it's about that. But it can also be about now. We can still have feelings, and for that matter girlfriends and motorbikes. So why not music? Music doesn't have to be a youth ghetto any more', I post, hopefully.

On the other hand, evidence that 50- and 60-somethings are in tune with now abounds. There seem to be plenty of promising profiles – self-portraits, put there for getting-to-know-you purposes – where potential GOMs can be found. Here's a 60-year-old 'ex computer engineer, ex roadie, ex playleader, ex draughtsman, ex builder of adventure playgrounds, ex several other things before being ex nurse', an activist in the health service with a wide taste in music who lists his hobbies as 'Fighting bureaucracy. Reading. Bringing up my youngest to be a free thinker.' And I like this dour

60-year-old Mancunian: 'Ageing rockstar who refuses to grow up. Also in development as a Spiritualist Medium – alas, these days I'm more like a large and I think my medium days are gone … Interests: play guitar, write, draw and keep computers occupied. Books: yup, got some of them. Likes: too much salt.'

I ask him, straight up, if he's a Groovy Old Man (without telling him what one is) and he replies:

'Now you're digging deep, aren't you. I'm still that seven-teen-year-old kid till I look in the mirror and find some fat, ageing impostor who's pretending to be me. Yeah, I've still got a lot of my younger attitudes – I played guitar in a band for 40 years or more on and off and that keeps you from growing old. But I don't like what I see in a lot of the new younger generation so either they're changing from what we did or I really am growing older and less tolerant – nah, that can't be it! So, no I haven't changed but the world has.' Promising. It's worth remembering that those who volunteer don't get admitted to the membership. And here is a refusenik with 40 years of music and a healthily wide perspective, even if he is a little concerned with his weight.

And here's a GOM-to-be, at 58, rugged-looking, wild-haired, grey-moustached, possibly on the pull (there's a lot of that going on) but with a philosophical bent. 'Tall, active male. I love life, and all the challenges it brings. My philosophy is always say "yes" then work out how.' He's interested in archae-ology, likes music of an eclectic mix from the thirties to the present day; has travelled widely and dislikes people who find it all too much to be bothered. And he's pictured with a half-made reconstruction of a historical building he's working on. I'm not suggesting that Saga Zone is full of GOMs. But GOMs and GOMs-to-be are easy to find, even if they tend not to be that communicative online. Elsewhere, it has to be said, there are plenty of elasticated-trousered, child-smacking enthusiasts getting together to discuss Saga cruises.

And it's on a cruise, oddly, that I find Royston Ellis, early chronicler of the British teenage scene, minor poet and major player in the game of fifties and sixties pop, and by email I explain my mission. By now things have got even more interesting with this chronicler of early pop, in terms of both his past and his present. In the early sixties on the island of Guernsey, Ellis introduced Lennon to a PVC-clad young woman called Stephanie, soon to be laminated into The Beatles' back catalogue as Polythene Pam. A possibly benzedrine-inhaler-fuelled three-in-a-bed shrink-wrapped-style rock 'n' roll romp may or may not have taken place. Royston Ellis may have been among the first to combine sex and drugs and rock 'n' roll.

Forty years later, he surely is a very groovy man indeed, and is described thus (http://www.roystonellis.com/):

'Royston Ellis was born on 10 February 1941 in Pinner, England, and educated at state school until he left, age sixteen, determined to be a writer. Two years later, his first book, a sequence of poems, was published and he performed his poetry on stage and TV to backing by Cliff Richard's original group, The Shadows ... Later awarded the title Duke Gypino de Redonda by the king of that Caribbean island. At twenty he left England for Moscow, where he appeared with the Russian poet Yevtushenko, and then to the Canary Islands where he acted briefly as an Arab with Cliff Richard in the movie *Wonderful Life*, and wrote three novels. From 1966 to 1980 he lived in Dominica, and wrote *The Bondmaster* series of historical novels as Richard Tresillian as well as becoming President of the Dominica Cricket Association, a member of MCC and of the Windward Islands Cricket Board of Control. In 1980 he settled in Sri Lanka. The author of over 60 published books he also writes travel features for inflight, international and Sri Lankan magazines.'

Having read of my mission, Royston emails from off Casablanca: 'Of course I am as groovy as I ever was, and still dapper, if fatter! I always thought that my feeling of being unlike the (British/American/European) men I meet of my age is because I escaped from the UK at age twenty and discovered a different way of life in first, the Canary Islands, then the Caribbean, and finally Ceylon where I live like a groovy neo-colonial.'

I hope this isn't entrapment. I haven't explained to him that over-enthusiasm is a disqualification. It's that final description that haunts me. It sounds like a Wonderful Life, all right, but are the words 'groovy neo-colonial' somehow a self-contradiction? Do we detect a tailing-off of style, culminating in becoming a member of the cricketing great and good? Off Agadir, Royston tells me he's on holiday and I have to wait a week for him to respond in full.

When he does, it prompts a crisis. Royston is keen to join

the Groovy train. But if music be the food of GOM, I'm worried about ingredients. He likes pre-fifties crooners and 'mood music'. Well, Burt Bacharach underwent a style rehabilitation recently, and I myself have Henry Mancini's 'Baby Elephant Walk' on my iPod. In my defence I stress that I have it next to 'Baby Genius' by The Eels. But pre-fifties crooners? Less sure. In a balanced diet of diverse music, fine. And there's nothing inherently wrong with pre-fifties crooners. Johnny Ray was, after all, David Style's entrée into the world of sixties freaks. And am I now donning the irrational wig and gown of Judge Mental? A crazy solution beckons: book a ticket to Sri Lanka and sample the lifestyle of the writer and expat – Royston has an auto-rickshaw and a driver, two houseboys, an estate manager for his paddy fields, a cinnamon garden, coconut and papaya plantations. And a cat. All of which, he points out, is much cheaper than a large flat in Brighton. And he contributes to the employment of twenty Sri Lankans. All Royston's wealth and style is based on pen power, which is all based on experience and derring-do.

In a long email he tells me how, living in early sixties Berlin, the Russian visa in his passport meant he could shuttle between East and West, carrying refugees' messages and possessions. It was he who suggested to John Lennon that the band should be called Beatles, not Beetles; in 1966 he fled from Spanish police on the Canary Islands having published a racy novel called *The Flesh Merchants*. He's been a docker, ferry boat engineer, TV interviewer, barman, actor. His life, from his 4.30am breakfast curry to his sundowners at Sri Lankan dusk, is his own creation, and although Tavy and the Teensters, Hazel and Babs, John and Pam and Cliff seem a lifetime away, they're all intimately connected with who he is now. A man with three dinner jackets (two black, one white) and a four-bedroom house full of antique furniture.

'While the modern generation dresses down, I dress up. My clothes are my own design with my safari suits tailored in Bangkok, my shoes handmade in Sri Lanka, and my boxers from France. I fly at the front of the plane on the principle that travelling in comfort in first or business class is better value than staying in a five-star hotel at the destination. I seek the most exotic accommodation, not the most expensive, when I travel, which is often. I have sowed my wild oats. I never did drugs, despite the nose inhaler episode recalled by John Lennon, and never married, although I fathered a child in Jersey in 1962 and have an adopted son from Dominica, Edward, who is partly Carib Indian and lives in London. I go to occasional parties but more often entertain at home where I get happily drunk watching the sun set over the horizon … If that doesn't sound groovy, I assure you it is! That's because I am my own master, doing what I enjoy.'

I don't even bother to phone the publisher of this book to ask if they'll pay for a trip to see Royston. If his life now sounds like an upmarket holiday, who am I to criticise? On the other hand, fifties crooners and mood music! I could go to Horizon Cottage and take my iPod. Reacquaint Royston with Jimmy Page, see what he thinks of the Led Zep reunion, try to turn him on to something more contemporary? But isn't musical style-repression damaging? A case in point: Matthew Bannister, aged 50 and an almost certain GOM-to-be, had, during his tenure as Radio 1 Controller, to be careful about publicising his taste for modern English folk music. It wouldn't have gone down well during the nineties Britpop boom. Now that's behind him he can, as it were, come out of the closet. Our first wave of Groovy Old Men never had a closet. In which case, why does Royston's musical taste seem so confined?

I decide, rather than eliminating Mr Ellis from my enquiry, to make a new rule. To confirm GOM status, I have to meet the candidate in the flesh. Inspired by this evasion, I nip down to my local street market, it being a Thursday, to see Paul, the youngest Groovy Old Man I talked to, born 1947. He remembers his music moment. It was in the back of a car, somewhere near Dagenham. He was sixteen. Most of his mates were into more commercial stuff. It was a rare airplay of 'Blowin' in the Wind', the Bob Dylan version.[13] 'And I twigged. I just knew it was different. I just got it.' His memory is very specific. The car was being driven by a mate. A trainee copper at Hendon. 'Not that it was common for me to have mates who were coppers', he adds, carefully. Oddly, the car was as important as the song. Ford Prefect. The old black cube body shape. Then he goes slightly wistful. 'Funny that. Hearing Bob Dylan in a car like that.' I know what he means, and he knows I know. The new design that replaced the boxy Prefect had

13 Peter, Paul and Mary had a UK hit with it in 1963.

modestly American styling. The old Ford Prefect is a pre-war design, discontinued in 1953, still common on British streets ten years later when Paul met Bob. It's a history moment, as well as a music one, linking the young Paul and the young Dylan with the past, the early sixties and the present. And even Paul, still Groovy after all these years, has a tick in the box marked music-maker. Back then he was a would-be lyric writer. A habitué of Denmark Street, the British Tin Pan Alley. And he nearly got somewhere with a song aimed at Herman's Hermits.

One GOM, asked by me for a classic track, a Desert Island Disc, one to remember, maybe even one for the funeral, chose *Arnold Layne*. Not one of Pink Floyd's best, even if it is one of their earliest. But who cares? Maybe it's a case of 'When I am an old man I will listen to Deep Purple.'[14]

14 With apologies to the poet Jenny Joseph.

CHAPTER FOUR

Music 1 Politics 0

'Street Fighting Man'
Rolling Stones

For a brief time, when Groovy Old Men were in their 20s or older, the 'counter-culture' meant both music and politics. They seemed indivisible. They fuelled each other. Enthusiastically gave each other credibility. The civil rights movement, the anti-Vietnam war movement, the black power movement had their anthems. The musical mystics enjoyed the same outsider status as the radicals. Rock 'n' rollers wanted to dress in the tough-guy image of revolutionaries. Revolutionaries were flattered by the attentions of men with democratic-looking leather jackets and big limousines. Liberalisation of the law on drugs was seen by both sides as radical and desirable. Yet for most of these men in old age, and the ones that follow, the music and maybe the drugs seem to have persisted, but the politics dropped away. The few that do have a connection with the radical sixties they experienced as 20-somethings – Groovy Old Lefties, we might call them – are oddly reticent about talking about their views. Some are single-issue activists rather than fully-fledged ideologues. Ray Gosling is a member of the Nottingham-based Church of the Militant Elvis Party, also known as the Militant Elvis Anti-Tesco Popular Front, whose main purpose seems to be to stop Tesco allegedly spoiling the Beeston area of Nottingham. But he was for years a key member and sometime leader of his local residents' association. Mike Bell, publican and finger-style guitar player, is that rare bird, a Groovy Old Conservative.

There's no such thing as a Groovy Young Conservative. Yet.

Ten o'clock in the morning in the front room of Peter Jenner's house, also his office. As a GOM sitting room it can't be beaten. It's lined with a distractingly diverse collection of rock and travel books and boxes labelled 'Party in the Park', 'Wiggy' and 'T-shirt archive'. Last night's DVD – a Chinese classic – on the coffee table. Jenner is recalling a key moment in his career, which spans academia, politics, music and technology, and he's hoping to start a technological music revolution in a later chapter.

'… and there I was refusing to publish my research because it would have been used by fascists and racists.' Jenner is describing a tight spot he found himself in. It was a crisis of conscience. His research into the economics of immigration wasn't at all racist, but it could be easily misinterpreted by those who were. This hurt Jenner a lot: 'I used to score my dope off West Indians. I loved black music.' At the same time, but for different reasons, he was refusing to mark exam papers, protesting against the academic board of the LSE, and about to have a music moment.

Jenner should by now be a politician, a journalist, a senior academic or some kind of economic or sociological guru. Maybe he should head a think tank. I'd quite like to make his story into a musical about the relationship between politics and music. Songs by Billy Bragg and Ian Dury. Message: Sixties teenagers took it more or less for granted that their political mood music should be left of centre. At the start of the sixties it was more likely to be men in their 20s who were seriously into both music and politics. These would later join the honoured ranks of the first generation of Groovy Old Men. Men, like Peter Jenner, with insight into both.

Peter Jenner was born in 1943. His father attended two hangings in the role of prison chaplain at Winson Green Prison. He'd been a strike breaker during the General Strike, a volunteer bus driver. But his experiences as a young vicar in Limehouse in east London sent him leftwards. In the war he was a conscientious objector. In 1943 Peter Jenner's mother witnessed a bombing. She was pregnant at the time. The bomb hit a bus. Very late in her life she told Peter she saw, at the scene of the bombing, a severed head rolling into the gutter. She thinks the shock of this had a physical impact on the then unborn Peter. He was born with club feet. His father thought the fact that he could walk, that he defeated this disability was, in a high church way, a blessing. Peter initially thought he was cursed.

Peter's theory is that the energy he would have put into

sport went into thought. In a pleasingly literal way, Peter has been there, done that and got the T-shirt, as well as being responsible for many T-shirt-generating moments. History with a capital H plays a huge part in Peter's present. A history shaped by the twin forces of 50 years of music and politics. History of a kind unavailable to future Groovy Old Men, except second-hand in books, movies, TV documentaries. Peter thinks he might just remember being taken to a hill above Bristol to see the lights going back on after the war. But he also thinks that might be a false memory, accidentally filed into the true section after much retelling. In other words, Peter is aware of the shaping forces of his personal history and how to decode them. One came in the shapely form of Dorothy Dandridge,[1] in the role of Carmen Jones, in the movie of the same name. She provided the ten-year-old Pete with his black music moment, though he says he also liked her because she was sexy. Peter's tastes were formed early.

I can't resist a nerdish impulse to link *Carmen Jones* with sex 'n' drugs 'n' rock 'n' roll. The story's all about sex. The music – not rock 'n' roll but certainly black/Bizet fusion – was experimental. The drug in the original work was tobacco. Bizet's Carmen worked in a cigar factory. She was updated to

1 In an unwritten chapter: Pin Ups for Groovy Old Men, Miss Dandridge is a high scorer. Not only for her beauty and talent, but also for her role in politics and an amazing back story in which she had a secret affair with Otto Preminger. And her mother was bisexual. Dorothy refused the role of a slave in *The King and I*. She was played by Halle Berry in a TV biopic.

parachute worker in the 1943 all-black stage musical, a celebrated movie of doomed love, boxing and all-American air force heroes. 'Beat Out Dat Rhythm on the Drum' and 'Hit Me with Your Rhythm Stick' are closely related. I hope the sex 'n' drugs reference won't seem too forced. Because Peter eventually became Ian Dury's producer and manager and has had a brilliant career in music.

There are scores of men in their 60s who have had non-guitar-toting rock 'n' roll careers in management, production, recording and A & R, all predictably Groovy, and all originally from diverse backgrounds. However, the distinguishing feature is that Jenner started his early working life in social theory. And although it was a chance encounter that led Peter towards music and away from politics and particularly economics, in which he has a first-class degree, he's well aware of the historical, political and cultural forces at play.

His grandfather had been a Labour MP. His clergyman father, when they moved to a Southall parish, used to get discount records from the local EMI factory, fuelling Peter and his brother's growing taste for jazz. He also wangled him into Westminster School, where Peter was an academic success but an institutional failure, his club feet contributing to his outsider and dissident status. Peter and his brother spent a while in 1960s Chicago, working in another patron-parishioner's whisky distillery. A city where they heard Muddy Waters and Miles Davis play. Peter Jenner knows where he was when J.F. Kennedy was *nominated* because he saw it on TV in the US, and supported Adlai Stevenson, seen as the more radical alternative.

Then the sixteen-year-old Peter went up to Cambridge. He didn't like rock 'n' roll. He didn't like Elvis. He couldn't hear what Elvis was singing about. He liked hearing the words. He didn't think white men could play the blues. He enjoyed the 'theological' discourse about jazz. Before the rows about Dylan going electric, Jenner enjoyed the arguments about whether it was OK to have the modern saxophone in a trad jazz band.

He'd be the ideal guy to mark your paper on the Battle of Beaulieu, observing that American culture embraces change, while British culture is prone to tribal punch-ups as a result of the unsettling effects of early urbanisation on a stable rural culture. Which is why the Dylan folkies didn't like him going electric. So here's Peter Jenner, at Sidney Sussex, Cambridge, 1959, club-footed dissident jazz and blues fan and intellectual, enthusiastically welcoming the physical female sympathy for his physical 'plight' and getting stuck in to the stuff of a subject which might help change the world for good. He gets a good first, then a research and teaching job at the LSE, where he realises that the work there was no more than 'an adjunct to the Labour Party'. This is at the birth of the academic discipline then called 'Social Administration' and now called 'Social Policy'.

Jenner's job was developing the software for Welfare State version 2.0. Known pejoratively by others as the Nanny State. Jenner points out that his generation still has strong links through their parents with the deprivations of the thirties. This at a time when attitudes to the Soviet Union weren't entirely negative, despite the disappointments of the 1950s.

The memory that the Soviet Union won the Second World War was still, in many minds, untarnished. Although everyone in Jenner's orbit was some kind of lefty, he had some basic doubts. 'I was becoming a deviant', remembers Jenner, using the word in its sociological context. The idea of 'economic man', humanity studied solely in relation to his or her material life, seemed restrictive. And the traditional assumptions of the welfare state were, he thought, being nibbled at, vulnerable to attack by a new kind of right-wing thinking, focused by the Institute of Economic Affairs. Jenner found that their most powerful argument, and one that needed a sophisticated response, was about work. 'If the welfare state was going to look after people equally well whether they were in work or out of it, where was the motivation to work?' was their question, and Peter found that the establishment pooh-poohed it with political pooh-pooh motives, rather than engaging with it practically, which is what Peter wanted to do. His heresy found its way into his lectures. He taught social workers the theory behind social policy, but he warned them that in their role as 'brain police' they needed to have some humility.

'What you're doing as a social worker is fucking with people's lives', he told them. 'You can't just come in as lord or lady bountiful and tell them what to do.' The real heresy was refusing to mark the students' essays and exam papers. His view was that there were no correct answers, a view that was both anti-academic and anti-orthodox left. That's not to say Jenner was seduced by the right. Perhaps his father's move from right-wing strike breaker to left-wing conscientious objector inspired

his heretical tendencies. Perhaps it was because political arguments were part of family life for Jenner. As an academic he
was getting interested in issues beyond the confines of pure
economics, asking questions about how economic circumstances relate to human happiness. His views on incomes
policy, a significant issue at a time of threatened inflation,
were also seen as heretical. He thought that increased immigration would hold wages down. It prompted a dilemma.
Publish and watch his work get hijacked by emerging right-
wing racists. Or don't publish and screw up his academic
career. So he refused to publish because he knew his work
would be used by the 'bad guys' as fuel for racism. It was a
decision that he knew would damage his academic career.
Another political fight along racial lines was breaking out at
the LSE, one in which Jenner was far less equivocal. In 1966,
Dr Walter Adams, a southern Rhodesian academic, had been
appointed by the LSE as director. Students and staff, Jenner
among them, opposed the appointment,[2] arguing that Adams
was a supporter of apartheid in his home country. At the
same time Jenner was getting more and more disillusioned
by the academic game.

Jenner had by then become part of the London Free School

2 In January 1967 a college porter died of a heart attack during a demonstration at the LSE. Students were suspended. There was an occupation
by students after it was revealed that the porter's death could not be
directly related to the demonstration. They sang 'We Shall Overcome',
the anthem of the civil rights movement.

movement, based in Notting Hill and peopled by dope-smoking white middle-class men in their 20s with good educations and similar doubts to Jenner's about a variety of orthodoxies. The only exception was Trinidadian Michael X, reformed strong-arm man for Peter Rachman, the notorious slum landlord, and soon to be the first non-white man to be charged for breaching Britain's new race relations law. Michael X was also a key figure in Britain's black power movement.[3] The Free School was a failure educationally – though the play group it helped to start did get a visit from Mohammed Ali, like Michael X a recent convert to Islam. Jenner found its most significant use was to look at how different disciplines might interact. For example, he could talk to psychiatrist Barry Miles about the psychology of economic man. And he could talk to a nuclear physicist turned photographer we will call John about travel. Or about dope. His North African connections were another unifying factor. They meant a steady supply of high-class resin for the Free School.

One Sunday afternoon in March 1966, Peter Jenner was up to his ears in marking. A pile of unmarked essays in the red corner were doing battle with the prospect of an interesting gig in the blue corner. It was a straight fight between rock 'n' roll and Social Administration. Music won. Sunday afternoon, with its Tony Hancock/Jimmy Porter associations of authentic British drabness, wasn't the best time for a gig. But the fact that it was at the Marquee was promising, and the musicians

3 He was later hanged for murder.

on offer had associations with the American cult band The Fugs. And although they played a standard rock blues repertoire, it was studded by long experimental solos, sometimes enlivened with the use of mallets. They were called the Pink Floyd Set. Thanks to Peter and his partner-to-be Andrew Blackman, the Pink Floyd Set's next gig would be All Saints' Church Hall in Notting Hill, a benefit for the London Free School. As Floyd's drummer Nick Mason points out, 'Like all good vicars' sons they knew that if you wanted to raise money, you either held a whist drive or a dance.'

The Floyd history is well worth reading at length.[4] But Jenner's history is more interesting. A-grade stuff, with roots in the stuff history does best. War, politics, shifting ideologies, deviance. Jenner chooses music, not politics. The journalist Nick Cohen says in his book *What's Left?* that the revolutionary 1960s had much in common with the revolutionary 1840s. They were 'failed uprisings that nonetheless had lasting and unintended consequences on culture and politics'. In a parallel universe, the unmarked essays win, Jenner doesn't see the Pink Floyd Set's gig, he decides to take on the Institute of Economic Affairs on its political home territory, Sir Keith Joseph sees the error of his ways, Margaret Thatcher continues her scientific studies and I'm now interviewing a Groovy Old ex-Labour minister who has hidden his Rizlas before my arrival. But music had more to offer Peter Jenner than politics.

4 And you can read it in Nick Mason's book, *Inside Out.*

So Peter went on to manage, among others, Ian Dury and Billy Bragg, artists with their socio-political hearts on their sleeve notes. Music's gain was politics' loss. Peter is engaging, far-sighted, unorthodox, attractive. And although he didn't pursue his career or act on his political views, he's still, in his mid-60s, applying historical and economic lessons to the music business, where he's spearheading fiscal and technological reform. We can't all be Peter Jenners. But back then, men in their 20s (and for good or bad, the prime movers were still men) could see the mid-sixties revolution in 3D.

Later in 1967, Jenner was walking up Oxford Street when he came across a load of kids with bells round their necks, hanging about UFO, the club started by Joe Boyd in Tottenham Court Road, and later frequented by David Style. And he thought 'Fucking hell, this is starting to happen. Unbelievable.' Had he asked those teenagers with bells round their necks to put the new found 'freak' movement into political or historical perspective, he'd have drawn a blank. He still might today, if he asked the 50-somethings they became. They were keen to get to the boutique called Granny Takes a Trip. But less interested in the trip granny and granddad had taken. Men of Peter Jenner's age, born before the historical divide that separates them from the boomers, were very well aware. And still are.

You don't have to have a degree in history or economics to have this authenticity. Market trader Paul, born 1947 and one of the youngest in the first wave of GOMs, has a shorter, equally telling historical anecdote. He's a small boy out for a walk with his dad, 1950-something, in the country. A shotgun-toting farmer stepping straight from the *Beano* book of stereotypes does the shouty 'get off my land' thing. Paul's dad, a Jewish veteran who'd fought the Blackshirts in the East End in the thirties and been a proud conscript in World War Two, is calm. 'You don't scare me', he says. 'I was in the Cameron Highlanders.' Half a century later, Paul, standing among his T-shirts, swells slightly with pride at the memory.

Tariq Ali is the embodiment of the kind of history that makes his generation potentially Groovy. In a way, he is the History man. In Hindustani, his name almost means history, as Enoch Powell once pointed out to him when they were political allies in the early sixties. Their brief alliance was on one issue only. Powell as a right-wing libertarian intellectual opposed Labour's early-sixties incomes policy as much as the 24-year-old left-leaning Oxford undergraduate. Ali pointed out to Powell that his Hindustani was a bit off target. Ali's name derives from 'taraqqi', which means 'progress'. Forty-two years later, I'm walking up Great Portland Street with Ali on our way to a radio studio. His other nickname, 'Street Fighting Man', was given to him by the Rolling Stones. It refers to his leading role in the anti-Vietnam war protest in Grosvenor Square that erupted in violence. Although I can't think of a man less likely to break out in a Great Portland Street fight.

Tariq Ali is the gentlest of men in demeanour and in debating style. At 64 he has lost none of the soft-eyed, soft-voiced charisma that helped make him a sixties icon. Although he'd rightly prefer to be described as someone whose political authenticity and consistency is beyond reproach. Both are true. Born the son of a socialist journalist and editor in Pakistan in 1943, he remembers his mother crying at the death of Stalin. Tariq himself wept on the death of Che Guevara, well before Che made his first T-shirt appearance. He had only just returned from the region of Bolivia where Guevara had been assassinated, when he heard the news. Rare among GOMs, he had no black music moment. His equivalent was a black politics moment, when he met Malcolm X. His opposition to the war in North Vietnam was fuelled by what he'd seen on a visit there, shortly after a visit to a Prague nearing its spring awakening.

The street fighting referred to by the Stones was the antiwar demonstration that took place in 1968 in Grosvenor Square, organised by the Vietnam Solidarity Campaign. The storming of the American embassy was the intention – though it was an intention never openly stated by Ali or others for strategic reasons. In a way it was an intensely symbolic affair. The American embassy was an impossible windmill to tilt at. Tariq Ali had promised Corin Redgrave to guarantee the safety of Vanessa Redgrave, who became a romantic kind of human battle flag embodying the hard left and at the same time good old British values. Mick Jagger was there too. The day after, British sympathies, as seen through the eyes of the press, were with the poor police horses, innocently trapped in the street fighting. There was no question that the symbolism went beyond protesting against British support for the war against North Vietnam. The Prague Spring and the fact that the mass dissent occurring around the Western world was powered by middle-class intellectuals and students rather than ill-educated drones was seen as threatening. As he walked towards the embassy, the Street Fighting Man was imagining a revolution that would take on Moscow as well as Washington. It was a big moment.

And it's worth remembering that, for a time, the idea that revolution might be more than just a hash-pipe dream was a cool one. The events in Paris, the rise of the left inside the Labour Party, making it Groovy but unelectable, the conflict in Northern Ireland, the emergence of radical feminism, attention-seeking bits of 'direct action' from the German ultra-left, the black power movement, and crazies like the Symbionese Liberation Army all led to a feeling that the centre could not hold. Even I, as a young drama student in Manchester in 1971, remember people singing, semi-seriously, 'As soon as this pub closes the revolution starts', which always made me wonder whether I was dressed warmly enough. This was a song from an agit-prop play called *Close the Coalhouse Door*, performed at a time when a lot of theatre was fashionably radical. One theatre company, 7:84, got its name from the ratio of wealth held in Britain. Seven per cent of the population had 84 per cent of the wealth.[5]

In his book, *Streetfighting Man: An Autobiography of the Sixties*, written in 1985, Tariq Ali regrets the period's place in

---

5 Meanwhile a box of, say, Terry's All Gold, an essential aid to theatre-going, was creeping towards the scandalous £1 mark.

cultural history as a time merely of 'happy mysticism'. 'I do not want to suggest that a Chinese Wall divided pop culture from revolutionary politics', he wrote. 'In fact during the high point of the movement there was a potent and heady mixture of both. We imbibed some of the music and devotees of the rock groups learnt a bit of politics.' But who benefited?

Answers are hinted at in the section of Ali's book featuring verbatim interviews and exchanges of letters with John Lennon, in which he explains some lyrics,[6] particularly 'Revolution', which unfashionably distances itself from direct action or street fighting and was criticised for being no more revolutionary than *Mrs Dale's Diary*, a domestic drama serial on the BBC Home Service. Writing 'Revolution', Lennon was in anti-combat mode. He wanted to be 'counted out' when destruction was talked about, according to the song. This at a time when the left was itself agonising about direct action, or street fighting, its sexier Rolling Stones description.

Later, Lennon hardened up a little under the influence of Yoko Ono, before entering his own 'revolutionary' period. It's never been entirely clear whether Mick Jagger attended the Grosvenor Square demo as observer or participant. One account has him watching from the steps of a house in the square. But the Rolling Stones had gained huge credibility from images of revolutionary street cool, on which they still trade today. And they're still no stranger to street protest.

6 Sadly, Lennon wasn't asked about the meaning of the then quite recent song 'Taxman', whose subject was a different kind of protest. His bill.

Why, only recently Keith Richards joined TV's Patricia 'Hyacinth Bucket' Routledge and actor Christopher Timothy, from *All Creatures Great and Small*, to protest about the changes to his local hospital where maternity and A&E services are threatened. Rock periodically needs to refresh the revolutionary tendencies it hatched in 1956 and 1968. Later, in 1976 it did it again; and in the early eighties it did it once more, before the establishment joined hands with[7] the music world for Live Aid.

Music connects men to the counter-culture era very powerfully. Women too, but in 1968 the early feminist movement had only just started. Then men were the moving force behind music, and its greatest commercial consumers. And, for the moment at least, they were the prime political movers. Now though, it's harder to find people umbilically connected to the era politically, and even the idea of left-wing theatre seems curiously dated.

However, Tariq Ali has managed to be totally consistent, still regards himself as a 'person of the left' (he avoids further self-labelling), while his career has taken him into fiction, filmmaking and radical journalism. It was his and Darcus Howe's *Bandung File* that exposed the BCCI scandal in the early eighties on Channel 4. He's found new hope in political developments in Venezuela. But there's a certain weariness about him when he talks about what happened to most of his fellow sixties street fighters. In his book he expresses disappointment and

7 Or stole the moral high ground from.

frustration at the way dissidence has been eroded. Channel 4, he feels, has lost its bottle, or sold it for advertising revenue. Rebels like the artist and film-maker Derek Jarman and investigative journalist Paul Foot are gone. Ali is currently experiencing more painful déjà vu because of the military coup in his native Pakistan. On the day I phoned him, right-wing historian David Irving and BNP leader Nick Griffin had been invited to speak at the Oxford Union about free speech. He sighs, eloquently.

I tell him that Dame Eliza Manningham Buller, until recently the head of M15, had chosen 'Street Fighting Man' as one of her Desert Island Discs on BBC Radio. It's the first time I have heard him cross. 'Jesus Christ, did she?' Ms Manningham Buller, born 1948, chose it to represent her sixties period, and explained her choice by saying she thought the Stones had more edge than The Beatles. She appeared to have no idea she was choosing a hymn to direct revolutionary action. She could have phoned a mate in the Service to look in Tariq's no doubt bulging file, but why should she?

Now as then, Ali is as likely to listen to classical music and opera as he is to listen to rock. And he does recall that Mick Jagger underwent a bit of a political conversion in the late eighties, becoming, like Lennon, a tax-fighting man and perhaps worse – a grudging admirer of Mrs Thatcher. But does he still think the 'heady' mix of music and politics he talked about in 1985 were indivisible? Ali points to the diversity of counter-culture causes: mysticism, marijuana, and soon after 1968 the huge expansion of the women's movement and gay liberation. It all happened at the same time. He seems less sure how well fused together it was. And though he regrets Jagger's move away from the left, he is encouraged by his more recent anti-Iraq war position. The factor that united all the factions in the counter-culture was opposition to the Vietnam war, seen every night on TV.

There's no question, Ali deserves full Groovy Old Man status, not only because of his authenticity and consistency and adaptability, his wide travels and his strong sense of history. I think back to Grosvenor Square, when, feeling like a would-be son-in-law questioned about his intentions, he had so gallantly promised the Redgrave clan Vanessa's safety on the demo. Shortly after, another young female star, Eliza Manningham Buller, was recruited into the secret service. When she joined in the seventies there were lots of women, but none senior enough to be considered able to, say, recruit operating agents. The reason given was that Russians or Arabs wouldn't have trusted a woman in that role. A consequence of the street fighting, though, was a start to the women's movement. These trends, with their roots in women's changing status and lives in two world wars, have been endlessly documented and evaluated. Women started to reflect about their place at the start of their fight for suffrage. Men stayed more or less the same.

Tariq has always felt betrayed by some of his fellow street fighters, once mainstays of the counter-culture, who now appear to have changed sides. At the mention of one name he changes the subject, tactfully but clearly. 'I don't want to talk about those guys.' This guy I mentioned to him also rose out of the student rebel left, a man who also nearly had his academic career abruptly ended when he protested against an academic being given a platform. Someone who 50 years ago told me in all seriousness that a lion lived in his garden shed. I could have dealt with that, except he made me go in the shed. There was no lion, but it was an unpleasant experience nonetheless. So while I have no hesitation in naming Tariq a GOM for his services to political consistency, I am concerned that I am withholding the title from the lion boy, the one Tariq wearily avoids discussing.

David, now Lord Triesman, is a distant cousin. It would therefore be inappropriate of me to either dub him Groovy Old Man or withhold that title from him. It's a pity, because I had the advantage of watching him grow up at reasonably close quarters. Had a Time Lord whispered into my seven-year-old ear, explaining that I would be writing this book some 48 years later, I would have believed him. Don't forget, Lord T (then just plain David) had had no difficulty convincing me about the lion. Had the Time Lord asked whether the then sixteen-year-old David would go on to become a Groovy Old Man, I, wise and trusting seven-year-old that I was, would have had little doubt. I remember a conversation around that time between Triesman and his father establishing that that particular evening David was going out to an event where there were to be GIRLS (my capital letters). David also was learning to play the guitar and had passed his eleven-plus with flying colours.

Nine years later, I'm sixteen, it's 1968 and David is in trouble. He has been sent down from university for allegedly being a

ringleader in an alleged violent attack on one Dr I.T. Inch, a
scientist from Porton Down, the government research establishment where it was believed chemical weapons were being
produced. David is part of a demonstration involving a mustard
gas bomb, although the mustard involved was I think of the
culinary variety. Sit-downs, teach-ins and other hyphenated
new-fangled protests follow. The entire staff of the university
chemistry department are surprised to see their jobs advertised in the national press, thanks to a prank. The press goes
wild. Eventually, David and his fellow victims are reinstated.

David goes on to be active in the radical press, joins the
Communist Party, then leaves, becomes a full-time official in
the University Teacher's Union, is made a life peer and in the
course of me writing this book, eventually moves from the
Foreign Office and becomes Minister for Students, or more
accurately, Government Spokesperson, Department for
Innovation, Universities and Skills. I'd like to ask him about
the relationship between the 25-year-old firebrand student
and the 64-year-old unelected Minister for Students. This
question would be naive and, as my mother points out, he is
my cousin, so such public wrangling would be unseemly. She's
the one who says you can't escape your background. If I can't
question Triesman in print for appearing to escape his radical
background, I can hardly have a public row with my mother
about her aphorisms.[8] Best if he's left unclassified.

---

[8] There's another reason why it might not be a good idea to consider him
for inclusion. See The Great, the Good and the Groovy in chapter six.

One candidate about whom I have no qualms when it comes to political interrogation about past and present is a man called Howard. Born lower-middle-class in the north of England, sociology graduate, you might remember him from the late sixties, early seventies. He was big in the seventies. So was his hair, his tie, his lapels, his trouser bottoms, his ramshackle house in a dodgy area of town – and his ego. His ego was huge. *You* know, he was early- to mid-30s, became a sociology lecturer at a campus university. Marxist. Taught sociology. Very of the moment. Shagged his students. Had no conscience. You *must* remember him. Droopy moustache, slight South African accent. He's a clear candidate for GOMhood, a child of his times, a bloke worth watching, a smooth operator. A populariser of radical thought, a feminist womaniser, a charismatically unfair teacher, a man who made people laugh a lot, a self-serving bully and a big success. Howard too famously led a protest against yet another alleged bad-guy coming to lecture at his university, a man called Mangel. Whereas Walter Adams – the object of the protest by LSE students in 1967 – was genuinely associated with the Southern Rhodesian apartheid regime, and therefore arguably a worthy target, Mangel, a Jewish social anthropologist with theories rooted in biology, seems pretty innocent. Howard, now in his late 60s, knows this as he knew it back then. Yet Howard was in the forefront of the rebellion against his invitation. In fact, it's pretty clear he *engineered* the controversial invitation in order to ignite the rebellion. And if challenged, I've no doubt he'd come clean about that, then come up with a slogan-explanation about ends and means. Eugenics and racism must be rooted out, and if mere personalities like Mangel are victims along the way, even if they are innocent, then it's just too bad. Ironic, that it's a biological theory that creates all this radical anger. Because what propelled Howard into the revolution in the first place wasn't rock 'n' roll or drugs. It was sex.

And I imagine Howard is pretty sexy today. With sociology fluctuating in the fashion charts, Howard, ever resourceful, has maybe written a novel. Created for himself a media career. Turned, suddenly in the eighties, to publishing, or PR or advertising. Invested. Owns a production company. Or a publishing house. He has, I think, three children and one grandchild by his first wife, and none by her successor, a modelling agent, to whom he is not married. As an after-dinner speaker he commands an £8,000–£15,000 fee. He appears on television and radio review programmes. He's still thought to be a bit of a ladies' man. His big hair has subsided to ambiguous-almost-no-hair, making it hard to tell through the tan exactly how much he's suffering hair loss and how grey he might be. But that's the idea. He'll laughingly tell you he gets the look in the shower with a disposable razor. It's so convenient. He has showers in the South of France, New York and London, where he's not too grand to go down the pub with former mates from his fifties grammar school past. One of this crowd wears big glasses and is called Alfie, though he's older than Howard by ten years. Retired with the proceeds of a successful minicab empire invested in abortion clinics.

He's unavailable for interview, sadly, because Howard Kirk is a work of fiction. Fittingly, he is *The History Man*, created by the late Malcolm Bradbury and immortalised by Antony Sher, the South African actor, hence the accent. And were Bradbury still alive he might, at a pinch, say with more conviction than I can what Howard Kirk is doing now, what *The History Man*'s history was over the past 30 years. He and his hair were big in the seventies. Is he as big, as it were, in his 70s? Is he a Groovy Old Man? What's it all about, Howard?

But soft! There's a way to get a bit closer to Kirk, or rather a Kirk contemporary. Professor Laurie Taylor, born in 1936, has a close connection with the History Man, as he explained on the BBC website:

'When it came out [in 1975], somehow or other, the story got around that the History Man was based on me. Indeed, I was a sociology lecturer, and I was associated with leftwing politics, and I suppose that I had acquired some sort of reputation at York University for being a little bit wild and a little bit libidinous. So people decided that I was definitely Howard Kirk. I used to try and deny it.

'Then I heard the television series was going to be made by the BBC with Antony Sher as Howard Kirk. I got a phone call from Sher, asking if he could come up and see me. I had to say: "Look, I've never met Malcolm Bradbury in my life, I don't know how the History Man could be based on me." He said he just wanted to see how a sociology lecturer conducted a seminar. So he came up, I conducted a seminar and he watched. When the programme came out, I was dreading it – I thought I'd have even more people saying: "You are Howard Kirk." Although I detected certain things in his mannerisms which were a bit like mine, I was really rather pleased. The *Daily Mail* hailed Kirk as a hero, an endearing chap. So all of a sudden, I was really rather popular – it was good to be Howard Kirk.'

And it goes without saying that it's good to be Laurie, celeb academic, broadcaster, journalist. Successful, brainy, urbane, and still capable of considerable enjoyment. It would be great to say that Laurie's political hinterland includes service at the barricades, the odd Maoist street-chant, or at least a sit down. As Professor G.R. Campbell recalled at Laurie's appointment as Doctor of Letters at the University of Leicester, the features that Laurie and Howard Kirk had in common included membership of the Trotskyist Inter-national Socialist Party. You can imagine Laurie rolling his eyes at this recollection.

But Laurie wasn't really much of a one for visibly rocking the boat. In a way, his first profession – acting – has coloured a lot of what he's done thereafter. He went from drama school to Joan Littlewood's radical Theatre Workshop at the Theatre Royal Stratford East. But his career was fatally pierced when a friend of his, a director, accused him of 'putting too much of himself' into his role. Actors are supposed to be empty vessels. His current job away from the Radio 4 microphone

– motivational and after-dinner speaking – includes skills honed as actor, salesman, librarian and comprehensive school teacher. And, of course, university lecturer. Like Kirk, Taylor revolted, but for proper academic reasons. Having studied both psychology and sociology as a mature student, the young lecturer got interested in criminology, then a discipline dominated by theory. Laurie, though, was interested in criminals, and befriended one, the bank robber John McVicar, with whom he wrote a celebrated book. That's not to say he downgraded the intellectual status of criminology or sociology. He just made them more interesting.

Taylor's favourite definition of an intellectual, by the way, is a person who can go into a room where there is a tea cosy and not put it on his head. As our conversation took place over lunch, not afternoon tea, this was as untestable as my theories about history, politics and Groovy Old Men. But although Laurie's history is colourfully diverse, and academically successful, intellectual seriousness in the shape of politics, history or sociology isn't his sole defining factor.

'For years as an academic I was L.J. Taylor, that's how I signed my articles and I was very serious and wore horn-rimmed glasses', he remembers over a pair of attractive-looking sausages. However, it was the appearance, he confesses, at the front of the lecture theatre of a leather-mini-skirted student with long legs and short black hair that, well, changed things. This was at the beginning of the seventies. 'The sixties were still going on', observes L.J., now Laurie, meaning that they started late and ended late, like one of Howard Kirk's famous parties. We can't identify the owner of the skirt, but she's now a big name in the arts.

The other shaping factor was also not politics. It came in the form of veteran radio producer, Hungarian émigré and confirmed tea-cosy-refusenik Michael Ember, who, encountering Laurie in his academic role, asked him to argue an arcane point from opposing sides. Laurie did so effortlessly, and thereby passed the audition he didn't know he was taking to be a panellist on *Stop the Week*, on BBC Radio 4. The rest, is History, man. For 30 years he has been running his own spoof university magazine, *The Poppletonian*, in *Times Higher Education*, the trade mag of the university industry, where he reports on academic and other matters – anything from social science to sudoku – which is probably, apart from the jobs pages, the most-read part of the paper. ('Following our Vice-Chancellor's CBE last year for services to the luxury travel industry, we were all delighted to learn that our very own Dr Harvey Cragg was a runner-up in this year's MBE list. Hats off to Harvey!')

What's impressive about Laurie is his breadth (his height, too). He can be serious, cerebral, funny, scathing, outrageous. An instructive suggestion: Google his images. His Ralph Steadman cartoon incarnation as editor of *The Poppletonian* is great. Here's Laurie's own description of Steadman on Taylor: 'My naturally broad brow has been given an extra inch or so and my cheekbones have been extended. My shock of hair is infested with flying bats and a large bolt has been driven through my neck. Not much ambiguity there. Thanks a lot,

Ralph. Every year I'm getting to look more and more like Frankenstein's monster.'

Yet his motivational speaker image online is very unFrankenstein. Short-haired, suited, often with a chin thoughtfully at rest on a fist, Rodin style. His delivery – breakneck speed, fearsomely passionate, arm-wavingly declamatory – treads a fine line between alternative comic (Alexei Sayle springs to mind) and military dictator. The Trotskyist has long gone, except perhaps in style. He must have been a hell of a teacher.

Laurie and music, though. Hard to say. He does vouchsafe over the sausages that he patronised the Merseysippi Jazz Band rather than The Beatles in the early sixties in his home town of Liverpool, but I suspect that was to demonstrate independence of mind. Encouragingly, Laurie is instinctively uncomfortable being defined as a Groovy Old Man. He's actually pretty uncomfortable being defined, I'd guess.

Don Wright, also a former teacher, is equally impressive, if not as well known as Laurie. He's the Tony Hawks lookalike from Sheffield, born 1945, who was that most reviled of people, a sixties primary school teacher. People often say to him that he's not normal. In a way Don Wright's working life was entirely political. He taught his kids the joys of finding themselves in diverse but always creative activities, usually including music and drama. He wrote plays with them and chose diverse but rewarding topics like the history of comedy, from Greek drama to modern TV. There's little question that Don quite naturally inhaled the political and cultural atmosphere of the time and exhaled it every day in class. Children's autonomy and creativity were at the heart of the liberal consensus, guided by the philosophies of Jean Piaget, whose theories placed children's personal experience at the centre of the learning experience. These were perfectly in tune with the post-war consensus that primary education could play a reforming role. A theory itself in tune with those who wanted a revolution. What better way to start than with a liberally educated, self-valuing, creative, free-thinking generation? The *Plowden Report into Primary Education*, published a year after Don started teaching, called for positive discrimination for the poor, special work with immigrants, more contact with parents, more male teachers, and a child-centred approach to education.

What people don't say about this kind of teaching is that it was, if done right, a lot of fun. And maybe what people see as 'not normal' in Don in his early 60s is that he took some of that fun home with him and still has plenty left. Don, among the first of a generation of guitar-wielding primary school teachers, is unabashed about the fact that he benefited from his time in the classroom. He chose topics in which he was personally interested. He developed some of the performing skills he now enjoys using in diverse bands. And, he says, creativity in teaching is often about being able to 'entertain yourself'. He hates what he sees as the prescriptive bossiness of the National Curriculum and got out of teaching before having to follow it. But he denies that his approach robbed kids of the ability to read, spell and do sums. 'I like structure', he says, and his book and record shelves, though groaning, reveal an inner tidiness at odds with images of hippy chaos. He taught reading, spelling and times tables as part of the whole package. What he doesn't acknowledge is that his motives and actions are in any way political with a capital P. He's voted strategically to keep Conservatives out of his area of Sheffield, but is more likely to vote Green than anything else, more as a gesture of support than because he thinks they'll win. And although he's a Green, he's not gloomy about the future of humanity. And he's got an allotment.

Not that this is supposed to be a career assessment of Don as a teacher. It's Don now I'm interested in, and maybe the abnormal thing about him is his rooted certainty. After all, it's Don and his ilk who have allegedly created a generation of ill-educated thugs (baddies always have ilks – why?). Don is unrepentant. All those years of teaching self-education to small children have paid off in his own self-education. Even if he refuses to link himself too strongly to the political atmosphere through which he grew. Although music is chief among his pleasures, he's a bit funny about it. His two loves, free jazz and English folk, are a bit of a mismatch for my taste. (Sorry, Don.) It's the only thing he feels sensitive about. He doesn't play his music to guests, because he fears he won't be able to stand their music when they return the favour.

Andrew Kerr is what Tariq Ali might call a 'happy mystic'. It's perfectly possible to join the dots between Kerr, the co-founder of the Glastonbury Festival, and Ali. Kerr's 1971 Glastonbury cohorts were 'Notting Hill hippies' from the same scene as the London Free School, where LSE political fugitive Peter Jenner was about to lay down his marking and take up with Pink Floyd, and where a protest against an academic appointment helped fuel the mainly Trotskyist student rebellion.

Kerr likes to be thought of as an 'anarchist'. Although banish all images of Johnny Rotten. He refers to himself as a 'Blessed Failure', which is also the working title of his autobiography. And he feels his blessedness in a deeply spiritual way. The autobiography promises to be a hoot, and Kerr has rightly spared this book only a short series of parps from it. So far we have met Kerr suffering public-school nastiness and non-commissioned/lower decks naval fun, both thanks to his then undiagnosed dyslexia, an uneasy mix with his top-drawer background. We meet him again in the late sixties in a pink corduroy suit, much admired by Princess Margaret. He's so far unaccounted for between 1955 and 1968. This bit reads like an Evelyn Waugh story.

The family farm in Oxfordshire couldn't support 22-year-old Andrew in 1955, so he was found a job in an advertising agency as a trainee account manager. At an early meeting to discuss a campaign, he asked innocently, 'Isn't it a bit dishonest to say that?' and a voice[9] Kerr describes as 'silvery and ambitious' said: 'I don't think you're going

9 The voice belonged to John Bowler from the eponymous hat family. Five years previously, the famous hat celebrated its centenary and was still widely worn.

to get very far in advertising, Andrew', a view with which Andrew agreed.

Andrew then went on to be a receptionist at the Automobile Association, a useful stopgap, and then, thanks to a chap he met in a bar, he was introduced to Randolph Churchill, son of Winston, and became Churchill's PA.

And now the spirit of William Boot descends on my tape recorder, a spirit of which Andrew and his publisher will approve, because the story fragments somewhat mysteriously at this life-changing junction in the Kerr political history, thereby preserving it for his autobiography. So this is how Andrew entered the Churchill fold in 1957:

'Eventually I saw Randolph and he said well I'd like you to join me on a march … … … … and so I … … … … … party trick … … … I saw somebody else doing the splits and my sister-in-law has … … and then eventually she's managed … … … she managed … … comedian … … So I met them and I was still in a state of not knowing anything about anything. Couldn't write, couldn't spell, just laugh … … … and anyway I had to … … … which I couldn't … …'[10]

Then, again for an occluded reason, after a year Kerr leaves

---

[10] Eventually I get a translation: Andrew's sister-in-law Iris, once married to the comedian Dick Emery, taught a teenage Andrew to do the splits. Later, Randolph Churchill asked Andrew to join his staff in March. Just before that date, Andrew drank half a bottle of brandy at a party where professional jivers were punctuating their routine with the splits, and Andrew decided to emulate them. His attempt at the splits landed him in hospital for three weeks. Thus delaying his employment with Churchill.

the Churchill employ and starts a real marine career, working on private yachts in the Mediterranean. This is where the already mentioned shipwreck occurs, but once more the information is patchy:

AK: No, I'm not telling you what the story is 'cause it's a fucking good story.

NB: Can we say where?

AK: Yes. Miles and miles from any land in the western Mediterranean. So it wasn't a rock job.

NB: A what?

AK: It wasn't a rock job.

NB: Which sort of rock job are we talking about? Rock 'n' roll, were you involved with touring?

AK: No, no, running a ship onto rocks.

NB: Right.

AK: Yes, and then it was at that time that I first smoked cannabis.

NB: After the shipwreck?

AK: No, before. Just before.

NB: Does this explain the shipwreck?

AK: No. It doesn't. You'll have to wait till the book arrives. It's a cracking good story.

Eventually Kerr pilots a ship back to Britain through the French and English canal system, paints houses, drives a minicab, and finally in 1962 returns to the Churchill fold. I don't think the reason for his leaving (or joining) Churchill was a political one. Kerr is – and was – blissfully apolitical in the orthodox sense. And he didn't seem troubled by the

conservative views of his employer, who was a highly individual man, often described as the black sheep of the family,
with the reputation for being irascible. He was an MP and
soldier during wartime[11] and afterwards turned to journalism,
though his own views on the press were highly critical. He
said straightforward journalism was being drowned in a 'deep
and lush and fast-flowing river of pornography and crime'.
His friend Evelyn Waugh, on hearing that Churchill had had
a benign tumour removed from his lung, observed: 'Leave it
to the surgeons to find the only thing that was benign in
Randolph and remove it.'

I'm interested in what it says about Andrew Kerr that this
apparently bad-tempered man, saturated in politics and
history, should be happy to have a dyslexic, unacademic,
unorthodox and slightly hapless personal assistant. Kerr
clearly sees him as a bit of a father figure. I think what it
says is that Kerr was, as he still is, immensely likeable and
highly individual with a complete disregard for conventional politics. He remembers how an office in the Suffolk
household of the Churchills was turned over to the writing
of Sir Winston's memoirs. Kerr didn't have a problem, politically, about helping to preserve the memory of this Tory
dynasty. Partly because a number of the researchers on the

11 There's a story that in Italy during the war as a member of the SAS,
Churchill and Evelyn Waugh were driving through a ruined southern
Italy. Churchill urinated openly in front of some ladies. Waugh asked
why. 'Because I am a member of parliament' was the explanation.

book weren't Tory either, and partly because he felt himself genuinely apolitical. He was heartened when Randolph told him that candidates in a parliamentary election had to read all the doubtful-looking ballot papers. Kerr then routinely handed in blank ballot slips. In 1966, when he accompanied Churchill to the US Senate, he remained strategically silent on issues like the arms race and Vietnam. If anything, Kerr inherited what he saw as Randolph's 'anarchy' without any trace of the aggression or political character. And he has been true to this, his social conscience developing much later on and uninfluenced by his former membership of the Establishment with a highly ornate capital E. It's worth remembering that this E and its proceeds built the foundations of the Glastonbury Festival.

David Style, born 1930, is apolitical too. Or at least, this is what he claims. He says he's a democrat. Yet he's been the most politically active, fighting fascism and communism. Of all the men featured here, he has the best record in street fighting. Political punch-ups. He'd done a bit of boxing as a kid, which helped, and in 1948 he joined the 43 Group, a loose organisation of mainly Jewish ex-servicemen and assorted lefties who had decided to put a stop to Oswald Mosley and his Union Movement of fascists. They were declaiming on street corners without fear of arrest that 'not enough Jews were killed at Belsen'. David's mob fought them on the beaches (or rather on the Level, in Brighton) and in the markets (Ridley Road, Stoke Newington) and they never surrendered. One or two went to prison, including David's good friend Barry. David shrugs at the notion that this might have been a political act. He was just a teenager, after all. 'I reckon it was just a chance to have a good bundle', he says. His Jewish youth club boxing had made him a bit tasty. 'I was part of a little team who fancied themselves. But if you're threatened isn't the best thing to fight back?' I remind him that only a few weeks previously Nick Griffin, British National Party leader, and David Irving had been invited to speak at the Oxford Union in a debate about free speech. Not that a man in his 70s should get involved physically, but didn't the sight of these guys exercising the right to free speech in the same way as Mosley, 60 years ago, make him feel like fighting back? He shrugs a bit. 'These guys aren't as anti-semitic as Mosley, or if they are they keep quiet about it.' Although the 43 Group were an important part of the fight against post-war fascism, David saw his part in it purely as self-preservation.

Twenty-five years later, it's the early seventies and David Style, then a family man in his 40s who has more or less foresworn photography and hippiedom and has gone into the antiques trade, steps onto the political stage again. This time it's the end of the military regime in Portugal and David had read *Death in the Afternoon* (Hemingway on bullfighting) and started to teach himself Spanish. So when his old friend calls with an idea for a Portuguese caper, David sees an opportunity to indulge his new-found Iberian interests. 'I wasn't interested in Portuguese politics at the time, all I was interested in was making some money. This was an exciting way to do it. And I understood the politics. And I despise communism as well as fascism. I am a democrat and a capitalist.' In Portugal in 1974 the long-lived 'fascist lite' military government had come to an end. It was eventually replaced by a revolutionary left-wing regime, the MFA, intent on nationalising financial and other institutions and collectivising agriculture. While America looked on in mounting horror at the possibility of a Marxist government in Europe, David Style and his friend Maurice could see some benefits and went into action. It was David who had introduced Maurice to the antiques business. Years later, Maurice had become an expert dealer in Oriental antiques and had fed the Portuguese rich's taste for exotic ceramics from the East. Wealthy collectors and traders in Portugal feared their collections would be confiscated. David and Maurice helped get them out 'quasi-legally'. The trick was to find English people with residential status in the UK, who were allowed to take out their possessions.

Operating out of 'safe houses', David and Maurice used fleeing English families as a cover for getting wealthy Portuguese people's riches back to England where they could be sold at auction. It was an endless round of hobnobbing with the posh Portuguese, bribing the Portuguese military and enjoying the sunshine and the scenery. In the end the cover story got thinner and thinner, with stooges being flown in to declare that they had been living in Portugal seven years. The British embassy turned a blind eye to the activity, the military and customs had to be bribed on the tailgates of the outgoing trucks, the goods were sold at auction, and the grateful Portuguese rich opened offshore accounts. David and Maurice took a cut from both the 'exporters' and the grateful auction houses. Give or take a gun pointed in the face and a nagging worry that they could be put in prison at any time, the whole experience was 'very pleasurable', made even more so by a handsome profit and a thrill that communism was getting a poke in the eye at the same time. But this was business, not politics. Asked to set the adventure to his own soundtrack selection, he is unhesitant. Velvet Underground and Pink Floyd.

So, what we learn here is that the political grounding of the fifties and sixties is a terrific aid to grooviness. Politics with a capital P was eventually to be ground out of existence. The romantic idea that anyone could change anything through what they believed started to look as threadbare as the donkey jacket that Michael Foot – who we remember being there at the birth of the Groovies – allegedly wore at the Cenotaph on remembrance Sunday 1981. Actually, it wasn't a donkey jacket; it was, by more reliable accounts, quite a smart duffel coat.[12] This proves the point about politics. It ceased to be seen as Groovy, as perception became more important than conviction.

12 The coat has a relevantly chequered history. Ray Brown (father of lad-mag-lad James), an expert on such matters and a grade 1 Groovy Old Man, made a radio programme about the duffel; 'a badge of membership of the left, a badge of the creative and a badge of those who didn't give a shit about bourgeois credentials', one interviewee said. Shame about the trad jazz connections.

Popular music, meanwhile, has hung steadfastly on to its anti-establishment roots. And Groovy Old Men have hung steadfastly on to popular music, while their politics might have drifted or diluted or disappeared. But rock and rebellion are still partners and always will be.

CHAPTER FIVE

Sex and Drugs

You make everything. Groovy.
Chip Taylor, 'Wild Thing'

Quite a lot of this is going to have to be anonymous, for obvious reasons. Almost all older men are sensitive about their current sex lives, and some, during the course of being interviewed, suddenly confided some pretty intimate stuff. 'When I was fifteen, I had my first sexual encounter with a Belgian policeman. Very enjoyable', said one. And here's another, Paulette the Tart, aged 60, who describes himself as a 'heterosexual maid' on a social networking website. He spends his weekends as Paul and his weekdays as Paulette, I assume. Initially, he agreed to be interviewed having sought permission from his 'goddess'. I have to assume the permission was withdrawn, because he suddenly went quiet. He's still very active online, where he can give his practice free, if silly, rein. But I get the feeling he quite likes the idea of also being able to discuss quite serious subjects online, while wearing (if only in his head, if it's a weekday) six-inch heels. A number of factors are at play here, some historical. First there's a long and grand tradition of transvestism made popular by Old Mother Reilly, Danny La Rue and later Paul 'Lily Savage' O'Grady. Second, Paulette may be too old to care. Third, his 'goddess' has been with him/her a long time, I suspect, so as well as being all rather naughty, it's in a context of being all rather comfy, if rather private. Ditto the drugs, where anonymity is concerned. A fair few of these men used and still use, and some, but not all, would prefer not to be er, grassed. And the drug use has passed, too, from the counter-culture to the comfortable.

That doesn't mean you have to be a drug-crazed transves-tite (or equivalent) to be a Groovy Old Man. It means you can, if you like. Usually in the privacy of your own home. Groovy Old Men may have been through a phase of dangerous promis-cuity and unsafe substance abuse, including alcohol. Now that they're older and wiser, it doesn't necessarily mean a monastic life. They can if they want and they do. Usually privately.

But just because what I've found out about Groovy Old Men is anonymous, it doesn't mean I've made it up. Mind you, some of the best made-up stuff rings true as well. Howard Kirk, for example, was a figment of the imagination so plau-sible that, like the best literary characters, he has outlived his creator. Otherwise I would have asked Malcolm Bradbury to do the honours and write a sequel. And although we can only speculate on Howard's status today, his entry point on the road to possible Groovy Old Manhood was in a way both sexual and musical.

Sex and Drugs

You may remember from the novel that, in 1963, Howard was working diligently in the library when a dark-eyed psychology student called Hamid called at the Kirks' to invite them to a jazz concert. Mrs Kirk and Hamid had sex in Howard's absence and needless to say the jazz was forgotten. The sex, though, was a liberating factor for the Kirks, and as a result they went on to experiment with pot, margarine, public nakedness and child rearing. At around the time of the missed jazz concert, Howard lost his father, 'the removal of the psychic focus of constraint', he called it, and gained a temporary assistant lectureship. Not for Howard the black music moment. I'm probably putting too much emphasis on the missed jazz concert. Sex was the personal catalyst that now makes Howard a GOM candidate, and propelled him towards being still, at 70, a sexy prospect when media folk are planning a chat show. Of course, we can't either grant or deny Howard GOM status on the same grounds that he can't be in a chat show. He doesn't exist. On the other hand, we might want to use him as a handy benchmark for men of this age for whom sex has been a significant shaping factor. Howard is almost entirely dick-led. Even when it comes to academic matters, his intellectual egocentricity is rooted in sexual conquest. Like his drinking buddy Alfie in the now smoke-free Fictional Arms, this makes him a compellingly interesting character, but not a very nice one.

On the other hand, one of the defining factors of Groovy Old Manhood is a certain magnetism. The suggestion that they might have put it around a bit. Are still attractive, capable of attraction or just capable. However, as many of them are currently in stable and happy relationships of one kind or another, poking about in their sexual pasts or presents is probably not a good idea. There have been revelations, reconciliations and regrets. So I am additionally grateful to those who have told all.

I heard one story about what sounds very much like a Groovy Old Man, the detail of which has to remain private. He had committed an indiscretion, confessed and been forgiven by his wife, under circumstances worthy of one of those TV dramas you see on Sunday nights. The telling element wasn't the story, the impact on the family or the response of the man. It was the look on the face of the woman, a family friend, when she told me the story. An indulgent smile. Not quite approval, but not disapproval either. There's an ambivalence about the idea of an old man with a past, just as there's an ambivalence about a certain kind of old man who might still be sexually attractive or active. A hint of attractiveness and the suggestion of continued capacity are important. It can still spill into a healthy disgust for the Steptoe-stereotype (Steptereotype?) of the disgusting old lech, but it doesn't have to.

Of all the factors, this one's the hardest to pin down. Old men can't all have the Paul Newman factor – twinkly-eyed beauty linked to a romantically supercharged past and a healthy salad-dressing income. What older men want now, sexually, is diverse in terms of quantity and quality. What they share is a familiar background of tolerance. Despite Philip Larkin, sexual intercourse began much earlier than 1963. Handsome Terry Shepherd 'screwing everything that moved' when he came out of the army in the late fifties, frustrated that the music scene had moved on while he'd been wasting time in Germany. However, the screws were rattled loose much earlier by the Luftwaffe, before Bill Haley or Elvis had sung a note. Ian Hobbs, for example, whose competence was so attractive to his newish partner Hilary, was shaped by a colourful mix of sex and history, which goes back to the uncertain days of the Second World War.

Ian's mother was an ambulance driver who got pregnant in 1942. Her inseminator then got a vicar's daughter pregnant and he chose the vicar's daughter as the object of his fatherly love, rather than Ian's mum. Ian was 'farmed out' till three, then came back into the family, where he and his mother were looked after by a married builder who set them up in a basement flat in Earls Court, and eventually lived with them. She opened a poodle parlour, Ian failed his eleven-plus, and mother, after an affair with a local headmaster who warned Ian away from his school, sent Ian to stage school. He had no choice in the matter and was soon one of a steady stream of kids appearing momentarily in fifties British films. Later in his teenage years he was expelled from drama school, after a disaster during a production of *Macbeth*. Lady Macbeth, then in her late 20s, was to be played by Barbara Moore, the singer from the Fraser Hayes Four, a talented musician and vocalist who was interested in straight acting. Maybe she wanted to get out of the Fraser Hayes Four, who padded out the comedy show *Round the Horne* on the Home Service with hit songs in close harmony style. The Four were largely resented for their interruptions of the radio fun, and not only by the audience. Kenneth Horne used to introduce them with lines like: 'And now with a hit from their latest LP, music to pick your toenails by ...'

But let us not make light of Barbara.[1] At the after-show party, Ian, whose description of himself was a 'green lanky streak of nothing', acted decisively. 'It was one of my better moves', he says. Barbara aimed a flirtatiously challenging remark at Ian. Ian, in a burst of romantic daring, swept her off her feet, found a lockable ante-room, performed a leading role, and the relationship – which Ian stresses became platonic – lasted ten years. 'It surprised a lot of people', Ian remembers with satisfaction. But the event was reported to the Corona management by Carol White, a student actress who would go on to be known for tumultuous affairs with A-list actors in Hollywood and Great Britain, as well as starring roles in British films of the sixties. Her motives were unclear. Ian had no reason to feel that she felt herself to be a woman scorned. Despite his triumphant, if fleeting, appearance as an extra in *The Prince and the Showgirl*, also featuring Laurence Olivier and Marilyn Monroe, the teenage Ian was 'too nervous' for big-time acting, so he got a job as an electrician at the Windmill Theatre. A mate told him this was a good job, not so much

1 Her great uncle by marriage claims to have shot Rasputin. She went on to a successful career in radio jingles.

for the sexual opportunities involved but because you weren't humping scenery around all the time and it was better paid than stagehandery. This was an important move. He liked life in theatres and studios as long as the spotlight wasn't on him. And he discovered that being in charge of the spotlight suited him. He found a talent for it.

Then, aged eighteen, he was discovered in bed with four girls from the Windmill Theatre, which despite the daringness of its nude shows had a reputation for strait-laced backstage discipline. 'It was perfectly innocent, sadly, I was unconscious with drink.' It was the morning after the night before and the dancing master (an odd job for a show in which the girls were required at the key moment to be static) arrived unexpectedly and caught them all non-flagrante, but Ian was fired on the spot. This injustice propelled him towards technical work in the mainstream theatre and eventually into the role of production manager and the effective practice of serial monogamy.

Serial monogamy – sometimes intensively practised but serial nevertheless – is more or less the norm for these guys, with a couple of attention-seeking forays into crazy promiscuity. Ian – perhaps because show business meant difficult timetables – explains that anything more complicated was too time-consuming. Above all, his history demonstrates how the forties and fifties were the key years in the sexual revolution. Sexual intercourse started in 1940, and was enthusiastically but quietly carried on in the fifties. The 1960s revolution that our young 20-somethings lived through was to do with sexual expression more than activity. There's a direct parallel here with music. The fifties saw a quiet DIY rock revolution, the sixties propelled it into the limelight.

Felix Dennis, poet and publisher, aged 60, is a hero in the struggle for freedom of sexual expression. In the sixties he'd had to sell his beloved Grundig tape recorder to fund a back-street abortion; and in *Desert Island Discs* (August 2007) asked us to thank the mid-sixties counter-culture of which he was a prominent part for the liberalisation of the abortion laws and for the first equal opportunities laws.

Dennis was a member of the trio that was convicted and imprisoned for 'sending obscene material through the post' and conspiring to corrupt the morals of the young, as one of the three defendants in the *Oz* trial, made famous by the movie *Hippy Hippy Shake*. The issue of *Oz* magazine in question was known as the 'School Kids' issue and was actually put together by real school kids in response to charges that the magazine's editors were out of touch with the younger generation. It featured explicitly sexual images of Rupert the Bear violating a young woman.[2]

Felix Dennis attended the committal hearing dressed, like his two co-defendants, as a schoolgirl. His conviction was thrown out on appeal and, as a direct result, the activities of the corrupt 'dirty squad' of porn-fighting detectives in the Metropolitan Police were exposed, culminating in a ten-year

2 Unfortunately, whenever a call centre worker says to me on the telephone 'bear with me', I cannot help this image recurring mentally.

prison sentence for the squad boss and pornography's move into the liberal mainstream. Fast forward 33 years to some more schoolgirl imagery, this time in Dennis Publishing's men's magazine *Maxim*, in which 'schoolboy crushes' are celebrated with the images of Tatu, the very young Russian pair of glamour models, and Gail Porter is dressed similarly to the on-trial Felix – as a schoolgirl.

Felix told Kirsty Young on *Desert Island Discs* that he missed out on fatherhood, but during his wild period in the eighties he had 'fourteen mistresses chasing him round the world'. And, perhaps oddly, he confessed to being 'not a very nice man'. He owned up to huge generosity, but explained his lack of niceness as due to his devotion to business and wealth-seeking, before asking for a stainless steel column for attracting 'mermaid pole dancers' as his luxury. I can't work out whether Felix is Groovy or not. It may be that he never fully grasped the modesty thing, and it may be that his self-demonising is just role play. He says he gets really angry at his shirts not being ironed but not angry when he loses $20 million in a business deal. He's an incredibly old-fashioned poet with a declamatory style recently compared to the hammily expressive Donald Wolfit, and comes across in interviews as a man with Something to Prove. Is he a GOM? Without meeting him it's hard to say. Childlessness, an absent father, a period of ten years of serious drug abuse also contribute to the image of the man, and some unkindly attribute much of his money-making determination to Judge Argyle's assessment of him as the least intelligent of the three *Oz* defendants. I asked his many press and PR people whether he was Groovy, after Felix decided not to be interviewed for this book. So far there has been no answer. So, in the absence of a personal meeting, the jury's out.

Groovy Old Men's sexual histories and the history of their sex keeps bringing me back to the early spring of 1968, and a house in Hammersmith. Vanessa Redgrave has just appeared as a cooler than cool model in the movie *Blow Up* and is soon to be Oscar-nominated for her performance as the crazily beautiful Isadora, both pre-lib sixties female icons. Wild thing, I think I love you. And here's GOM-to-be Tariq Ali, summoned like a nervous groom-to-be to the house by brother Corin. Corin wanted to ask not about Tariq's intentions vis-à-vis Vanessa, but simply to guarantee her safety on the anti-Vietnam march to Grosvenor Square. The Redgraves in 1968 were iconic. Father Sir Michael was identified with pipe-clenching British rectitude in films like *The Lady Vanishes* and *The Dam Busters*. Sister Lynn, also present at the Vanessa safety meeting, is best known for her performance as a ditzy dolly bird who learns to know her own mind in *Georgy Girl*.[3]

Had the protest taken place a year later, this meeting couldn't have happened. Tariq Ali would never have been summoned to the house in Hammersmith because Vanessa Redgrave wouldn't have needed male security. The women's liberation movement – which had been on the move since protests over women's suffrage – had been given added and sudden impetus

3 James Mason plays the lecherous tweedster who tries to 'buy' her.

by the sixties counter-culture. The widespread protests against Miss America and Miss World pageants were on very public display. Tariq Ali's magazine *Black Dwarf* was soon to release a women's issue. The Equal Pay Act was passed in 1970, guaranteeing equal pay for equal work. Employers would have a generous five years to comply. Confusingly, at almost exactly the same time and thanks to the reverberations of the very same counter-culture that brought you equal opportunities and eggs thrown at Miss World supremo Eric Morley, pubic hair in men's magazines would become visible for the first time.

For teenage baby-booming males, born in the late forties and fifties, these seemingly contradictory images of what women were, what they did, and how they were viewed might have seemed a bit confusing. Their older brothers in their 20s, the Groovy Old Men-in-waiting, had been witnesses to the tail-end of National Service and the start of rock 'n' roll. They had jived with, then twisted with and probably slept with Hazel and Babs or equiv. Some, like Paulette, had decided to dress like Hazel and Babs. They had perhaps experimented with benzedrine inhalers and 'purple hearts' as well as the drugs that came after. They had jobs. Many of them had kids. Perhaps this made them better equipped to deal with the apparent contradiction between sexual liberation Felix Dennis style and the outcomes of the women's movement, both of which sprang from the same root. But a lot of them were too busy with work and family life to take much notice.

What adds to the attractiveness of these men now is that

they almost all became hands-on fathers, so they know how to relate to children and are good grandfathers. The reasons for this are diverse. They saw the value of having more to do with their kids. They saw the value in women's arguments that said they should be more involved domestically. They and their families started to see the benefit in an extra income. They wanted to play their kids' guitars.

Attitudes to children generally changed for the better. Adults and kids could have fun together. Some of my men had witnessed the 'new man' trend, and the rather short-lived and self-conscious 'man's movement', which attempted to re-evaluate the role of post-feminist men. Some of the lessons learned from this were clear-cut and worth thinking about: how new male–female roles at work might mean new male–female roles at home. Some of it was enjoyably if risibly based on the 'mytho-poetic' ideal of returning to an imagined primitive manhood where anger and fear didn't rule, but ritual did. This involved going into the woods and drumming. It was a North American idea, but Epping Forest or equivalent stood valiant service in the UK.

One (now old) new man remembers attending a men's conference at which the idea of a generalised male 'monster' was discussed, the familiar Mr Not-nice-guy, horrible brother-in-law/nasty neighbour sort of bloke. The traditional, tried and testosterone way of dealing with this guy was, of course, combat. This could take the form of anything from arm-wrestling to chess, pub quiz or pub car park brawl.

These new men decided the best course of action would be to assuage feelings of antagonism to the monstrous male stereotype by dressing a tree trunk as the monster and then making ritual sacrifices to it. Obvious really. But the following day at the final hold-hands-in-a-circle conference plenary session, the poor male monster was left outside for obvious reasons. He was a tree. Our participant thought this was wrong. He thought they should have gone outside and said goodbye to the tree/monster. Allowed it to feel included. Which means somewhere in Britain there's a very confused tree,[4] forced to adopt the role of male monster, then receiver of sacrifices.

Ian Hobbs, *Titanic* survivor and Windmill Theatre bad-boy, doesn't strike me as the kind of bloke who would be interested in this sort of thing, although he is a father par excellence, in terms both of quality and quantity. In his case, after his wife died he found himself working at home when he started a furniture design business with his new partner, and that meant being more with his children. Having had seven, he was pretty child-friendly. Now, his new partnership with Hilary means he has a hand in care of some of her kids as well, which he enjoys. Only David Style, born 1930, confessed to being distracted by his 1960s hippy life, meaning that he wasn't at home as much as he should have been. By that time

---

4 At about the same time, John Wells and John Fortune co-wrote a book satirising new-found sexual freedoms, about a man who had sex with trees, *A Melon For Ecstasy*. ('A woman for duty, a boy for pleasure, a melon for ecstasy': Turkish proverb.)

his business was starting to decline and he admits to a certain selfishness, driven by the drugs and music. Now he's making up for it by being employed by his son and being a super-grandad.

We seem to have strayed somewhat from the being-found-in-bed-with-four-Windmill-girls scenario. The sex in the chapter title is looking a bit forlorn. But sex also means simply being of the male sex. Over the GOM lifespan that has changed a lot. Part of being Groovy is the ability to ride with those changes. A lot of my subjects say they get on very well with young people and kids – in fact, the only age group they have a consistent problem with is their own. However, for the Windmill fans, as it were, early on in the book a female observer said she was attracted to her GOM partner because of his 'competence' and it's almost a platitude that men who are good with kids are often attractive to women.

The nearest I can get to a conclusion on this subject doesn't seem very Groovy. Baldly, serial monogamy makes Groovy Old Men relaxed. I asked one of my subjects, who admits to making a hash of his nuclear family life, with his partner going off with a 'younger richer man', whether he would like a new female companion. His 'yes' was wistful. Ray Gosling has got a new boyfriend, a roofer, having lived with his friend Bryn for 30 years and devoted himself entirely to Bryn's care over a long period when he became ill and eventually died. Peter Jenner, a widower, has hooked up with a lady who was a childhood friend. I'd like to think that Groovy Old Men – after a lifetime of sexual adventure

– continue in the same vein. The trouble is, it might not be true.

It might be true of future GOMs, but they'll be different. Applicants for the status of next generation of Groovy Old Man are preening themselves in the wings of the next chapter. (I've warned you, if you try too hard, you don't get in.) However, there's one vital change which I think might affect their status, so listen up, guys, and put those combs away.

In the seventies, there used to be a TV commercial in which a lovely woman passed two city gents. 'Is she, or isn't she?' one bowler-hatted gent asked the other. Pay attention, please, the point will become clear, although at the moment these gents' interest in the lovely woman seems entirely prurient. Is she or isn't she *what*? Those who remember having *Crossroads* interrupted by this commercial will know the answer: 'Is she or isn't she wearing *hairspray*?' The point of this ad was ambivalence. When Hazel and Babs took to the dance floor twenty years earlier, the answer was almost certainly and overtly 'yes'. Hazel and Babs's hairstyles were intensively sprayed, sometimes with light aircraft. Openly and without a care for the threat of global warming. But by the time the seventies and this commercial happened, spraying became a less acceptable practice. Not because of greenhouse gases, but because fashion decreed that hair should have a more natural look. The point about this particular spray and commercial was that it made the lovely woman look as if she might *not* be wearing any artificial aids to tonsorial tumescence. And that rather posh knob-gag is a clue to what I'm on about. The very existence of this brand of hairspray, the commercial claimed, made it impossible for others to know whether she was or not. Of course, it would be rude of the bowler-hatted blokes to ask whether she was using hairspray, but the 'money shot' from the commercial confirmed she was, because you saw the canister poking out of her handbag.

Now, you there, applicants for the status of next generation of Groovy Old Men, preening yourselves in the wings of the next chapter: would anyone care to say why the Harmony hairspray commercial is symbolic of your sexual futures? No? Clues: 'tonsorial tumescence', 'knob-gag'? Absolutely right. For hairspray, read Viagra. Much of the current coverage about Viagra features younger men currently using it entirely recreationally, even though they might not 'need' it. They use it to prolong and enhance enjoyment, in the same way that other less legal drugs, starting with the content of nasal inhalers, are used to prolong wakefulness and stimulation. As these recreational users age, many may continue to take Viagra, and take it for granted. You can imagine a commercial of the future, probably Dutch and introduced by an ancient Chris Tarrant or similar, with a lady wondering 'Is he, or isn't he?' And not asking the gentleman in question, for the same reason the blokes in bowlers kept quiet in the hairspray commercial. In other words, the stigma of sexual dysfunction among older men will in the future disappear in a blue cloud of Pfizer-powered performance. Before we hear a muted hooray from the wings of the next chapter, a pause for thought. This trend possibly makes the future less bright for the future GOM. It's possible he'll feel a 'duty' to perform. He'll be less in touch with his own libido.

This may be a very male point of view, and it's worth remembering that women are initiators and choosers too. Emma Soames, editor-at-large of *Saga* magazine, points to a recent Saga survey that says that sexually transmitted infections are on the increase among older people because many of them are back in the dating game, but few are bothering with contraception. The use of Viagra is part of that picture. She smilingly imagines some women in the future 'frog-marching the men to the chemist's, or more likely to the General Practitioner for Viagra, an image which somehow doesn't look that Groovy to me.

John Reilly is precious. Of all my guys, he's the one who spoke most candidly about Viagra. He's the 70-year-old who organises book launches, fashion shows and media events in still-fashionable Notting Hill. He has tried Viagra, but didn't like it. 'It felt like fucking with someone else's dick', he observed. This means he'd prefer to use his own. To choose the natural path. And, more or less free from the pressure of having to take Viagra for granted, he doesn't.

Simultaneously, John is Precious. He's precious because he seems to have got it sorted, the way he feels about his sex life, past and present. And Judy Garland named him Precious. She was watching *Bewitched* one day in 1966 when a character called Precious reminded her of John. The name stuck. When I started on this endeavour I didn't expect iconic names of the 20th century (Winston Churchill, John Lennon, Judy

Garland, Kenneth More, the Fraser Hayes Four) to have come into contact with my guys, but they have been useful, to say the least. In 1966, through a friend of a Californian friend, Miss Garland hired John as a minder. Nothing could have broadened his mind more.

The son of a wealthy concrete manufacturer, John says an early influence was the movie *Mame*, with wacky Rosalind Russell living life to the full ('Life is a banquet, and most poor suckers are starving to death') and damning the consequences. Whether John identified with the flamboyant aunt or the impoverished nephew she adopts isn't clear. The fact that he's inspired by the exploits of a mature, pleasure-seeking woman might be significant. Maybe it was because she was a contrast to the reality of his alcoholic mother. I'm sure John has thought of this. He was a psychology graduate who later became R.D. Laing's assistant, and after that a psychotherapist and counsellor. After he'd helped Judy Garland, that is.

John had grown up and studied in St Louis where, as a student waiter, he had watched the early performances of Barbra Streisand and Woody Allen. By the mid-sixties he was a surfer student, blond and I suspect beautiful, if a little innocent. This is the young guy who gets handed a tablet by a girl so beautiful he takes it then asks her what it was. LSD. He's a very calm, relaxed man at 70, so maybe he was the same at 28. Unflappable. At his interview, Miss Garland greets him in the full clown costume and make-up from *Easter Parade*. John is unflapped. He gets the job. Which seems to entail diluting her vodka and adulterating her barbiturate capsules with baking powder, and being unflapped by her gay entourage. He accompanied her to seedy drag clubs, where at the end of many a transvestite homage to 'Over the Rainbow' she would fling off her sunglasses and headscarf and reveal herself, to camp cries of amazement and delight. Some nights John would take her to the men's dorm at UCLA in the small hours of the morning to play pool with students. Or Tab Hunter and Rock Hudson would show up for a specially chosen screening. John asked her why she chose a straight minder, rather than one of her adoring gay followers. 'They steal my jewellery', was the tart reply.

As a finishing school for socio-sexual education, the job couldn't have been bettered. Later in the sixties, with the American dream repeatedly shot to pieces, John, like many other young Americans, fled to Europe, ending up in Rome. He was hired as a film extra by, among others, Federico Fellini, and he soon learned that blond hair was very saleable. He started an extras agency called Blondes, which did very well. He thinks he might have been one of the first owners of a credit card in Rome. It all sounds a bit like a novel featuring Mr Ripley. Except John isn't the murdering type. Mind you, his neighbour in picturesque Trastevere was a young actress called Sharon Tate, who was shooting a movie called *The Thirteen Chairs* with Orson Welles.[5] She was just about to return to California and she invited John to go with her, to keep her company 'while Roman shoots his movie'. John declined, narrowly missing an encounter with Charles Manson.

5 And Tim Brooke-Taylor. Interesting casting.

Now John's working full-time, just 70, having lived in Britain since the late sixties. He confesses to a 'low boredom threshold' (and a fear of fat people, which is probably irrelevant) and works in a glamorous industry with glamorous people less than half his age. In a world where personal relationships are prized, he happily plays the father figure or big brother role where appropriate and 'doesn't hit on' inevitably younger women colleagues. I find this a telling statement. Not so much because in my opinion men approaching 70 usually do 'hit on' younger women, but because John felt he ought to tell me this. Maybe the implication was he could hit on them but doesn't. Maybe it's just frankness.

Like many a Groovy Old Man, he was already an experienced 20-something when the counter-culture put sex on its front page, and he had the additional benefit of being rich, handsome, American, and with an insight into psychology. All of which seem to have stood him in good stead. He had a twenty-year marriage between the early seventies and the early nineties, which produced two sons, who he sees all the time. He and his ex-wife are on very good terms. One of his sons, now in his 30s, is possibly not his son, biologically. 'Of dubious paternity' sounds Victorian, but it's a good description if the doubt isn't weighed down by moral judgement. The possibly natural father is a wealthy friend living offshore, but John raised the boy. The situation is openly acknowledged in this extended family. Nobody has ever seen the need for, or wanted to have, a biological test. John's nine-year-old grand-daughter glories in her excess of grandfathers.

Now John is in a relationship with a wealthy 64-year-old Cuban-Italian woman who, when we met, was on a trip driving vintage cars around China. Sex is less on the agenda now, which John says is a good thing, believing that it leads to an unhelpful possessiveness. He laughs at the story of Kingsley Amis's relieved reaction to the departure of his libido, likening it to being unchained from a cretin. But I get the feeling John hasn't entirely welcomed the uncoupling.[6] He's still an open-minded kind of guy when it comes to both sex and drugs. All the same, now, if a beautiful young woman offering a tablet approached, I suspect John and others would think again. Groovy Old Men like reliving their careless pasts, but their presents, for the most part, are pretty careful.

For example, in 1971, Andrew Kerr was funding and setting up the Glastonbury Festival. One spring afternoon at Worthy Farm, just after he had taken some LSD, he remembered he had agreed to attend an important tea party with the local member of parliament and others. He was a little concerned that he might not acquit himself well at the tea party, and cast about for some help. And there, coming towards him, was the competent-seeming David Style, former photographer, antique dealer, Nazi-basher, weekend freak and all-round man about town and country. No surprise that these two

6 Groucho Marx, vintage GOM, publicly regretted the passing of his powers. In later life he is reported as saying: 'I'm going to Iowa for an award. Then I'm appearing at Carnegie Hall, it's sold out. Then I'm sailing to France to be honored by the French government. I'd give it all up for one erection.'

should know each other, though they haven't seen each other for a long while, now that Style has abandoned Glasto as 'too poncey' and Kerr has retired from active festival service. Back in spring 1971, David was part of a coterie of weekend hippies, many from Notting Hill, who were there to help. David's job was to source the free vegetarian food from local producers. Just before the acid kicked in, Andrew asked David whether he'd mind accompanying him to the MP's tea party, as a safeguard. 'Sure', says David. 'But I think you should know I have just taken some mescaline.' Cue falling about giggling both in 1971 and again 37 years later when it's remembered independently by both.

Despite the carefree pasts, many of the men I spoke to independently voiced two concerns about current marijuana consumption. One, concern for current youthful users about the increased strength of what's on the market. Two, concern for themselves about how to use it without using tobacco. One uses herbal tobacco, a number grow their own or have access to home-grown products of trustworthy weakness, so adulteration with tobacco is not needed. It's worth noting that very few are tobacco smokers. Lots still drink. One or two a lot. One, who lost a child, preferred drink to drugs as a preferred oblivion method. A few experienced marijuana before its fashionable appearance in the sixties counter-culture. Those closely related to the roots of the counter-culture (Tariq Ali, Peter Jenner, etc.) were witness to the way an authoritarian response to illegal drug use helped seal its popularity. The best-known manifestations of this were the 1967 prosecutions of rock stars, notably Jagger and Richards, followed by the appeal for tolerance in *The Times* in which William Rees Mogg quoted Pope's 'Who breaks a Butterfly upon a wheel?' But earlier that year, a less well-known figure, John 'Hoppy' Hopkins, had been sentenced to nine months' imprisonment for possession of an amount of cannabis that would nowadays probably merit a caution. His mistake was to plead not guilty and then try to defend cannabis as harmless from the dock. Hopkins was one of the founders of *The International Times*. The Metropolitan Police was riddled with corruption and keen to be seen to be fighting iniquity; the establishment hated *The International Times*. It was Hopkins', not Jagger and Richards' sentence that originally provoked such a strong reaction. The first generation of Groovy Old Men know this. For many of them, rolling a joint is still as much a ritual anti-establishment gesture as a means of enjoyment. Future, history-less generations may not feel the same way.

It's hard to say whether drugs will lose their anti-establishment cultural sheen among new Groovy Old Men. Those for whom drugs have been a rebellious gesture for 40 years aren't going to be swayed by establishment-led anti-drugs campaigns. Maybe ethics will, for future generations, eclipse rebellion. The same people who care deeply about the comfort of their dinner-party chicken know little and care less about the cost of the line of after-dinner coke in terms of Central American crime, murder and corruption, or destruction of the rain forest. One traditional 'stoner' Groovy Old Man argued that it would be better for Afghan heroin-poppy farming to be supplanted with marijuana, though how that might come about in practice is difficult to see. Of all the Groovy Old Man candidates seriously involved with drugs, Felix Dennis stands out as the man who independently went cold turkey because his huge crack cocaine habit was getting in the way of his equally huge money-making habit.

All Groovy Old Men will have come into contact with illegal drugs. If you're 70 and were never in a room where someone used drugs, it's doubtful you're a GOM. That's not to say by any means that using drugs or having used them is an entry requirement. A couple I talked to tried recreational drugs and found they didn't like the effects. A couple just said 'no'. A number had periods of abstinence from all intoxicants, alcohol included. But none were censorious about drug use. Some actively support legalisation. Again, that's not a requirement. Sadly, I'd guess that men are – and continue to be – more closely related to the drugs culture that started in the fifties and sixties than women, possibly for historical reasons. It may be worth noting that Howard Marks (born 1945) has no female equivalent. And my estimation is he's not very Groovy, because after the description 'former dope dealer', what's left?

CHAPTER SIX

Stairlift to Heaven

'Dedicated Follower of Fashion'
The Kinks

Paul Smith, aged fifteen, laid out the corduroy trousers carefully. Next to them, a checked shirt. Using heather he'd gathered on a cycling trip across Derbyshire moorland, and a photograph of a rural scene taken by his amateur photographer father, Paul created a little display. Painstakingly, he lettered a caption in pencil, 'Country Tweeds', and the name of the warehouse in which these were for sale. An undiagnosed dyslexic, Paul spelt it 'Wearhouse'. His boss was intrigued, if a bit mystified. This was a wholesale place, trade only, so Kenneth More was unlikely to drop by, tap out his pipe and replenish his supply of corduroys, however enticingly laid out the merchandise. The year was 1961, before Paul Smith accidentally collided with the art school world and the sudden sixties boom in men's fashion. This display was just Paul being Paul. His dad once took a photograph of him in Skegness. In it, eleven-year-old Paul is wearing a pale beige raincoat, and his dad has created a caption this time: 'Smart from the start'. His dad was a 'credit draper', selling bed linen and men's shirts door to door. He was a fun guy, too, a photographer, sketcher, joker, a 'card'.

Now Sir Paul's clothes are worn by Mervyn King, Mick Jagger, Stephen Frears, Ray Gosling, Tony Blair. And a lot of young chaps too. Broad appeal. And he does girls' clothes as well. His is a delightful success story and he a delightful bloke. Bloke, definitely. His office on an anonymous edge of Covent Garden is a stunning example of tasteful blokehood. Big, rectangular, dominated by a big rectangular walnut conference table and stuffed with stuff. I felt I wanted an hour with Paul and then an hour with the room. Lined and piled with neat shelves and columns of books and CDs, bicycles and photographs, sculpture and paintings, just a lot of great stuff.

Accident of birth may have made him heir to his father's aesthetic. A bicycle accident in 1964 ended his sport cycling days. Had it not been for that, Sir Paul might now be running a top cycling store, or chain of top cycling stores. A pal he'd met during three months in hospital suggested they have a drink in the Bell Inn in Nottingham. It was Paul's first drink. But the greater, stranger intoxicant was the atmosphere that emanated from the art student clientele in the pub. It was the excitement of their language more than the strangeness of their clothes that got him interested. Becoming a Groovy Old Man became unavoidable. He went into menswear, first as an assistant, opened a shop in Nottingham, then in London, then around the world. Today he's dressed in a pink-and-white candy-striped western shirt, the pearly buttons rectangular in shape and all differently coloured. His own brand of designer jeans. Greyish horn-rimmed glasses that give him the air of a literary academic, but one who loves his work, judging by the smile that beams through them. Not surprisingly, he's huge in Japan, where old age is venerated (not that he's *that* old, born 1947), as is hard work, Britishness and good design. Personally, Paul has democratic views on ageing. His dad died at 94. He's just had lunch with a former colleague, a man who ran a suiting factory, who is also in his 90s. Mind you, he's just had lunch with the T-Mobile cycling team. I get the impression he can have lunch with pretty well whoever he likes.

The point is that he doesn't really care about age. And when it comes to his menswear collection, people are more likely to ask him why he doesn't make clothes for fat blokes, rather than why he doesn't make clothes for old blokes. In fact, he caters for both but makes neither a special case. One factor that he does find defining is Britishness. Or perhaps undefining would be more accurate. In Italy, for example, a male item that becomes fashionable – he cites a quilted waistcoat – will be adopted by the president and the local cab driver. 'Whereas in Britain we're into doing our own thing, it's more of a conversation, more diverse …' This may have something to do with the variegated effect of the sixties, during which Smith was creating for different pop tribes. In the eighties, he was designing for yuppies, whose youth and diversity may have been at odds with their jobs. In the City, suddenly the subject of media fascination, the eighties revolution meant adjustments to expectations of public-school background and pin-stripes, while maintaining an atmosphere of monied good taste. 'A bit of colour in the check; a bit of colour in the linings of suits; coloured socks …'; the revolution was a quietly male one. In all, Smith has helped sow and sew the seeds of many a future Groovy Old Man.

But his success is based on a formal masculinity of the kind that refers back to the pre-pop era. Sure, he did the odd ripped T-shirt in punken times, but he's given to staid old wood panelling, is Paul. The fittings of his London shop still have something nostalgically conservative about them, lots of wood and glass-fronted drawers, which make the clothes leap brightly out at you. The foyer of his London HQ is lined with wood panelling rescued from an old Paris hotel, for example. And while I wait for him, 50 beautiful teenage girls, impossibly thin, impossibly tall, troop noisily through for a casting. They enter, check in, shed flat shoes, put on impossibly high heels, talk a lot, some in Russian and Polish, are ushered into the casting room, then out again. Shed high heels, don flats, etc. etc. Many carry a mobile phone and a packet of ten fags which will fit into skinny jeans. Smith, don't forget, now designs for women as well as men:

'When I eventually designed clothes for women it was a big problem for me because I don't have that feminine side, and a lot of fashion designers for women are gay and have a strong feminine side to them, and are interested in old movies with Katherine Hepburn and their hair and make-up and aware of the latest models. I have to be aware of all that because it's my job, but I like architecture and photography and cycling and normal boys' things so it was more of a struggle for me.' Smith's brand of masculinity, bred and grown between the eras of Kenneth More and the Kaiser Chiefs (current clients) is typical of Groovy Old Men. That's not to say Groovy Old Men can't be gay or for that matter anything else, in terms of their sexuality. It's to do with being at ease with yourself and understanding where you came from and how you got here. And what you're wearing can be as much an expression of that as what you eat, read, watch, listen to.

I produce a short Groovy Old Man fashion parade in my head. It's headed by David Style (by name and nature) who likes western shirts, quality leather jackets, hats, two-tone shoes. Very smart casual in all. Next on the catwalk, Terry Shepherd. Denim and T-shirts, silver designer jewellery, and the leather jacket that was part of the ensemble that caught my eye and eventually my imagination. Now, Andrew Kerr, Glastonbury co-founder and king of the compost castle, who poses a problem. From the waist down he is standard Groovy. From the waist up, a tweedster. Black-and-white tweed jacket, yellow shirt, neckerchief. Not cravat, I grant you. The neckerchief is a bit louche, but has something of the fifties about it. Kenneth More might wear it for sailing. From the waist down, however, Andrew wears combats 'n' Converse basketball boots. Universal, relaxed, could be a seven-year-old or a 70-something. It reminds me of those double-flap picture books where you could select permutations which included a policeman from the waist up and a ballet dancer from the waist down.

The rest file past in a blur of jeans and T-shirts, trainers and sweatshirts. Like new blokes Chas and John. Both are white-bearded – John rangy and fit-looking with neat zippy cardigan, combats and shoes that look like leather trainers. Chas wearing the universally ageless male uniform of jeans and sweatshirt with the look of a twinkly-eyed marine uncle. At first I confess to having been disappointed with John and Chas. It felt like I'd gone all the way to Liverpool on a wild GOM chase. Nice enough blokes, though. Relaxed, chatty, good-natured, long-retired central heating engineers, they ticked a few of my boxes (no National Service, some rock 'n' roll), but the GOM count seemed low on the face of it. There had been no four-in-a-bed romps with showgirls, they'd never done drugs, their contact with heads of state, stars of stage and screen or Rolling Stones had been zero. The closest either ever got to fame was when Chas's girlfriend appeared fleetingly in the dancing crowd on *Oh Boy!*, a 1950s rock 'n' roll TV show. Of course, both know someone who knew The Beatles before they were famous, but all Scousers worth their salt have a maximum six degrees of separation from the Four.

Chas (born 1938) paints. John (born 1940) started an oral history website about Liverpool, having always been interested in history and having taught himself computers. I guess that John's the more methodical of the two, Chas the more adventurous. They both hike. John's the more serious in terms of exercise, but they both go to the gym. John's training for a 10k charity run. Chas got into amateur dramatics – he's practical and artistic, making him useful as set-builder, but he does walk-ons as well. They both had a bout of being extras in films and TV together, but the hanging about got to them a bit. In the end, John was asked to shave his beard off so he could appear in a photograph as a murderer's father and he refused. He didn't mind being a murderer's father. He didn't want to lose the whiskers. Chas's father had been a merchant seaman who ended up skipper of a Mersey dredger. John's father had been a Regimental Sergeant Major who later turned to selling power tools on the markets.

Chas has travelled widely, both do the odd driving or handyman job if called upon. John spends a lot of time on his website, which is where I came across him. Neither is particularly political, Chas is a small c conservative, John a floating voter. He confesses a sneaking admiration for the achievements of Liverpool's 1980s militant-led council – he spent a lot of time fitting central heating in the growing number of newly built council houses in and around Liverpool. All the same, he disapproves of the radical means the left-wing council under Derek Hatton used to get them built.

For some reason we get into a conversation about whether, if we'd been the Tom Courtenay character in *Billy Liar*, we'd have taken the plunge at the end of the film and gone off with the Julie Christie character. Billy, you remember, was a compulsive fantasist and reluctant pen pusher in a firm of Yorkshire undertakers, but he had aspirations to be a comedy writer. At the end of the film he has to decide whether to join Julie on the late-night train to London, where possible fame and fortune beckon, or stay in his safe humdrum world. Billy,

John and Chas are almost exact contemporaries. Chas – marginally the less Groovy-looking – runs off with Julie without demur. John's not so sure. In the end he decides to reject her and the London life. The *Billy Liar* test (try it at home with grandad!) prompts an hour of soul-searching about male independence in the fifties and sixties. Both men were forbidden motorbikes as teenagers and didn't feel fully independent till their 21st birthdays. John thinks his maybe rigid background might be responsible for the break-up some 30 years ago of his first marriage, making him more flexible for the second. Then, touchingly, he talks about how towards the end of his life his father willingly reversed father–son roles with him – acknowledging John as the 'authority' where he felt it appropriate. Now, John's learning new skills – the skills of a housekeeper. His wife's had a stroke and is partially disabled. He approaches the unfamiliar world of housework with the same practical mindset he approached central heating and computers. Neither Chas nor John had much experience with practical domestic matters, and neither did much hands-on fathering of small children. 'Apart from occasional bathing', Chas adds, somewhat pedantically.

The other important thing about Chas and John is the length of their retirement. They've been retired for over twenty years, having planned hard. John, especially, had had enough of staring out at a constipated M62 through the windscreen of a British Gas Transit van. He knew all anyone needed to know about central heating. The planning for the next stage in their lives was entirely financial. They didn't give the massive increase in disposable time a second thought. No leisure workshops for them, no need to list their interests and hobbies. Now I feel guilty for being disappointed with Chas and John – because these guys are eloquent if subtle proof of the theory. They didn't need me to come and point out to them that they're nothing like the old men they encountered in their youth. They had realised this already. And they made me realise that early retirement, possibly a disappearing factor in the future of GOMhood, is very common among their generation, giving lots of older men time and space their predecessors never had, and their successors might have to do without. And both are keen to stress that history didn't exactly pass them by, but they were very busy fitting gas boilers and feeding children during the counter-culture's most heated years. They agree they're nothing like a lot of their contemporaries in their late 60s and early 70s. They have this in common with a lot of Groovy Old Men. Apart from carefully chosen friends, they aren't that at home with a lot of their own age group. Their friendship spanning 40 years or more has been crucially important. This is another factor I may have so far missed – the ability to maintain close, like-minded long-term friendships – and it sets me thinking of David Style, still mates with his fellow-adventurer from the Portuguese importing affair. Then I'm reminded of Paul, the market trader who nearly wrote a hit for Herman's Hermits. He told me that every Wednesday he and two long-term mates of his age have dinner in a local vegetarian restaurant. I ask if I can gatecrash. The look on Paul's face says 'Forget it'. Sacred territory, the Wednesday nights.

The most important thing about Chas and John is that their trace elements of Groovy Old Manhood have accumulated through a long period of osmosis. I stumbled more by luck than by judgement on a lot of the other guys, with their glamorous connections and showbizzy anecdotes. Chas and John are in a way remarkable for being not that remarkable. Except that they're a kind of proof.

In the vanguard of the movement are the flamboyant, carefully dressed, occasionally drug-fuelled, formerly highly-sexed adventurers, whose close shaves, brushes with stars, political and musical stories, dimly remembered encounters with Hazel and Babs and good-for-their-age good looks make them worthy trendsetters. It brings to mind sitting in David Style's comfortable-boho front room. We've had a cup of herb tea, he's shown me one of the vintage western shirts he collects, combing the trendy second-hand clothes stores off Brick Lane. All the while, he's breaking off to program his wife Marion's mobile phone so it will do predictive text, to take work calls, and then to kiss and cuddle a needy granddaughter, one of a bunch he and his wife look after regularly. This kind of child-care has become a standard role of the modern grandparent of dual-income kids and I ask him whether he feels forced into the role. He has confessed to me before he'd like to travel a bit more, but for his commitments here. But the answer's a firm 'No'. Grandchildren rule OK.

Meanwhile, Marion's patiently struggling with tiny boots and coats in the hall, and I feel slightly guilty for knowing all about her husband and not much about her – except, perhaps, that patience might be chief among her virtues. I know enough to know she's kind and gentle, patient and generous, but I feel uncomfortable going down the same avenues with her as I've been with the men. Reflecting on whether she's 'good for her age' (she is) or what kind of 1960s she had. But is she a Groovy Old Woman? Once again I find myself asking whether there is such a thing. 'Old woman', whatever the context, sounds harsh. For example, I know an old woman who swallowed a fly. And another who lives in a shoe. Whereas 'old man' can at least be a term of endearment. Joni Mitchell's old man, Lonnie Donegan's 'My Old Man's a Dustman'. Best stick to the men, for the moment.

Once again I stress that many of the men here are carefully collected rarities, products of a time of low birth rate, high expectations, great music and intense historical change. With them are the contemporaries whose jeans and combat trousers and sweatshirts we take for granted, because a lot of us younger chaps are dressed the same as them, have some similar tastes in music, the same outlook. They're still quite Groovy in their 60s and 70s, still independent-minded products of a half-century of amazing history, still with diverse taste in music (Amy Winehouse, by the way, scores well among 60- and 70-something men) but less flamboyant than the star guys for reasons explained by Chas and John. Work and survival took up a lot of space. These men are not so noticeable because older men aren't that noticeable. But they are worth scrutiny.

Behind them the youth cadre, GOMs-in-waiting, now in

their 50s, the baby boomers. A far greater proportion of these will quietly aspire to be Groovy Old Men, and a good number, provided they don't try too hard, will succeed. Some of them will have made arses of themselves in late middle age, and will find it hard to recoup. And none will have the authentic glamour of this first wave. That's why many in the second wave seem so keen on the music of their seniors. Reunions of Led Zeppelin, The Beach Boys, Madness, The Groundhogs, Squeeze, The Who and others have all happened while this book has been under way. Not to mention the Bonzo Dog Doo-Dah band.[1]

What the second wave *will* have that the first wave doesn't is a habit of self-examination based on a sixties teenage and an exposure to the commercial culture that they took and still take for granted. A media-conditioned concept that is totally alien to those in the first wave.

Lifestyle.

Sorry, let me put that in inverted commas. 'Lifestyle.' Really this word needs more than punctuational handles. It deserves to be behind bullet-proof glass, in the dock, on the bonfire,

1 In fact, best not to mention them. They cancelled their Xmas gigs due to mysterious unforeseen circumstances, and original member Legs Larry (born 1944) Smith appeared on Radio 4 to read an explanatory prepared statement. Unfortunately this was less than helpful as the statement seems to have got confused with a 'lifestyle' shopping list. *Racing Post*, strawberry jam, etc. Concern was centred around bass player Vernon Dudley, born 1933. In June 2008 David Style and I went to see them. They played two hours to an audience of enthusiastic Groovy Old Men.

or rammed up its own arse, if it had one, because that's where it belongs. It doesn't have an arse because it doesn't exist. Lifestyle, heretoforward used disdainfully but without inverted commas, is a made-up sociological-sounding word used mainly to sell people things, by trying to make them think they're a certain 'type', predetermined by all-colour magazine features. The things it most often sells are magazines and TV shows, which then go on to try to sell people more things. But the guitars, western shirts, painting materials, gig tickets, CDs, houses, bicycles, mobile phones, books, computers, Rizlas, combat trousers, car stereos, Converse footwear, Viagra and compost-making machines owned by my guys are not part of a single, consciously-lived style of life. They're just stuff they've bought. Terry Shepherd's fascination with modern jewellery, David's shirt-fetish, Andrew Kerr's obsession with compost, these are nothing to do with anything they've read in a magazine.

But insofar as magazines and other media depict a world they take to be that of their readership, I feel compelled to make further enquiries. It's at the offices of a magazine that I happily find myself in a lift with a key Groovy Old Man-in-waiting, Mark Ellen. A nice-faced fellow with a winning smile and an important history, Ellen, I suspect, might be less than pleased to see me at the HQ of *The Word* magazine. First and foremost, Ellen is an accomplished journalist, so he possibly – maybe rightly – mistrusts the attentions of other journalists. Ellen's importance starts with his former member-ship of what may be historically but certainly not musically the UK's most important rock band, The Ugly Rumours. Front man T. Blair. Blair himself is a knowing icon for this and future generations, and his training with Ellen and the Rumours, and before that briefly as a would-be rock promoter, helped shape the image of the prime minister-to-be. The photograph of Mr Blair going in and out of Number 10 in the familiar public-school combo of jeans and suit jacket, guitar case in hand, is an important one. Forensic decoders of spin always pointed out that when he's pictured like this, returning perhaps from family travels, you never saw him holding a briefcase or torn duty-free carrier full of used tissues, junior Calpol and bits of Lego. Others carry that for him. But the guitar case is an eloquent lifestyle statement aimed at three generations of voters, particularly male ones.[2] So he carried it himself.

Whether Blair receives a GOMhood in five years or so isn't important. Mark Ellen, who went into journalism after the Rumours, certainly will, and not just for being an Ugly. It was he in the mid-eighties who recognised a gap in the market for a 'more intelligent' British rock magazine, and was launch editor of Q. For 'more intelligent' read 'older'. But the 'O' word was then, and is still, largely banished from magazines related to pop music, for intensely traditional reasons. It's a lifestyle thing. Music buying has to be portrayed

2 PM Blair received gifts of guitars from Arnold Schwarzenegger, Mexico, Fender and Bono. Under rules governing gifts to ministers, these had to stay at Number 10, in the care of Gordon Brown.

as part of a youthful lifestyle, even when it isn't. However, twenty-odd years ago Mark Ellen realised that 40-somethings in the eighties could have their youthful cake and eat it as part of a sensibly balanced older lifestyle, which included kids, steady relationships, work and – here's the clever bit – increased income. This meant that *Q*, with its ironic Brit-banter house style, could chronicle past and present pop and give equal weight to both, all the while advertising cars, hi-fi, cameras, fags and gig tickets to a profitably wide age-demographic that took in wealthy older men. Young readers bought *Q* for its intelligence and older readers bought it in order not to have their intelligence insulted. All this, look you, without the use of the dreaded 'O' word. Pop used to be part of a youthful phase, as Giles Smith so pithily observed in his 1995 personal pop-quest *Lost in Music*, 'now it looks as though youth was just a phase pop music went through'. Ellen, brilliantly, spotted this.

Ellen and his close associate David Hepworth even invented, as part of a pitch to advertisers, a lifestyle subgroup called 'Fifty-Quid Bloke'. Initially, Hepworth used the term to explain in turn to the warring HMV/Virgin empires that Mr Fifty-Quid, tie askew after a few post-work drinks, was magnetically attracted to record emporia, where he thinks little of filling his wire basket with £50-worth of purchases. The guilt occasioned by the fact that he doesn't have to scrimp and save like he did as a kid is easy to assuage. He starts by justifying that bit of Mac software as work-related, buys something for the kids, then for Mrs Quid, and finally for himself. This at a time when older people, predominantly men, were accounting for more and more album and live performance sales, and the record companies began to concede that the over-40s had been poorly served by the music industry.

Even Fifty-Quid Bloke, conceived in 2003 as part of the ad-sales pitch for *The Word* magazine, is starting to age. In the five years since he was invented, he has seen the light and turned to downloading rather than buying. He doesn't have to have the CD in his hand any more. He's grown out of that. He might be thinking of his pension, a second home, whether he still wants to have sex with his wife, or worrying about the nagging pain in his back. But he certainly doesn't hope he dies before he gets old.

All this talk of ageing is why Ellen might be less than keen, initially, to talk to me, a person who uses this word with abandon. Because the 40-somethings he appealed to with such flair in the mid-eighties with *Q* are now 60-somethings and gaining. I suspect he might be worried that I'm going incontinently to use the 'O' word loudly in his office. Suggest, even, that he puts more explicit 'O'-rated content in his mag, which is almost an 'O'-free zone.

A glimpse at *The Word*, aka 'Intelligent Life on Planet Rock', bears this out. Ageing and old age is tangentially rather than explicitly dealt with. Here's a feature about DJ Steve Lamacq (born 1965), well known for going to gigs seven days a week to spot the next big thing, fuelled only by a teenage diet of crisps, fags and fizzy lager. Will he still be doing this when he's in his early 60s, asks *The Word* pertinently. 'I'll carry on doing it until I wake up one morning and discover I've fallen in love with trad jazz', responds the smart Lamacq. Note the use of trad jazz here as synonymous with old-fashioned naff. So we'll take that as a no, then. Elsewhere, the reviewer Joe Muggs daringly introduces a club music compilation CD by observing that *The Word* reader probably doesn't go raving till 5am all that often, and taking it upon himself to introduce readers to the joys of soul jazz. And of course, the usual battered icons appear regularly in some form or another, as they do in other mags like *Mojo* and *Uncut*, inspired or created by Hepworth and Ellen, aimed at an 'intelligent' (euphemism for older) audience: The Beatles, Dylan, Joni Mitchell, Springsteen, Robert Plant, Led Zep, Roy Hattersley, Michael Caine, comforting presences for the senior fans who don't get out much these days, bless 'em. Ah, wait a minute, here's someone new, or rather someone old without being cosily familiar who's also new – an ancient white bluesman called Seasick Steve.

Seasick and his story reek of authenticity. How much of this is the authentic kind of authenticity, rather than PR-type authenticity, is hard to say. A new festival favourite, he's a white country bluesman, hobo-hippy and former bill-sharer with Lightnin' Hopkins and Son House. Seasick is a living Woodie Guthrie whose story will have wide demographic appeal, especially among an age group for whom authenticity is prized above novelty. He's also, the piece claims, a survivor of Seattle-based Nirvana-related grunge, handily sealing his potential appeal among younger listeners. I even read about him in *Saga* magazine, the lifestyle magazine for careful older drivers. Mind you, Mr Sick does live in a caravan, which might increase Saga interest levels. For caravan, read elasticated trousers, vitamin supplements and eventually, stairlifts. And wait a minute, the piece about Seasick Steve in *Saga*, expressly for 50+ people, was written by *The Word* editor Mark Ellen. I mention this to Ellen's close colleague, David Hepworth. Until this point, Hepworth, Ellen's friend and co-Mr Fifty-Quid inventor, has been unflappable in the way that only a former *Old Grey Whistle Test* presenter can be unflappable. However, asked whether *The Word* readers might react queasily to authentically Groovy Mark Ellen slinging his hammock alongside Seasick over at the overtly 'O'-rated *Saga* magazine, he has to think a bit.

Ellen, it turns out, is comfortable with this double life being known. He doesn't care if *The Word* readers see that he's flirting with the elasticated-trouser lifestyle. He emails, about *The Word* readers: 'Those over 40 are thrilled to find a magazine that sees the world the way they do, and doesn't make judgements based upon how voguish anything might be. And isn't making them feel uncomfortable or left behind or trying to make faces behind their backs … We're just like that second cousin you always look out for at the family wedding, the one who wants to nip out into the garden for a fag, a light ale and a load of amusing banter about obscure rock 'n' roll bands.' A *cousin* at the family wedding, let it be noted, not an older relative, not an uncle or grandparent. It's an ageless, loose-agenda approach that *The Word* is aiming at – an agenda to which modern marketing practice is very slowly being attracted, and one way to explain this is by torturing a frog. Boiling it alive.

Here's what you do. Take a frog and a very large cooking vessel full of cold water. Place on cooker. Put frog in water. Very, very slowly bring up the heat, till the water boils and the frog dies horribly. Don't worry. This is a story from the marketing industry, so it's very colourful but it might not be true! It's an allegory. To make you feel better still, the frog represents a 20-something brand manager of a commercial product. The kind of product that isn't age-specific, so not denture-adhesive or alcopop. Frog, aged late 20-something, has to decide how the media is used in the promotion of this product. His or her instinct is to give it a zestily youthful image in the hope that young people buy it, like it and keep buying it till they die, 50 years later. Also because he or she is zestily youthful. Job done. Trouble is, being a young brand manager is demanding work. The meetings. The paperwork. Not to mention scanning the recruitment pages of the marketing press for new, better brand manager jobs. All the while, and slowly but surely while little Mr or Miss Zesty has been thinking of other things, the buying power of the old has increased, like the temperature of the frog water, while the buying power of the young hasn't, because they are getting more and more skint and can't afford to rent, let alone buy. The slow increase in temperature goes unnoticed by the fast-living youthful marketing-frog, so by the time he or she starts to feel the heat, it's too late to get out of the pot. Let alone the kitchen. Our marketing person is locked into campaigns aimed at the young.

I think the frog analogy applies beyond the strange world of marketing and PR. Groovy Old People, especially men, are only slowly becoming visible. Back in 2004, when Fifty-Quid Bloke was new, Tim de Lisle wrote in *The Guardian*: 'One of the ancient laws of rock concerts states that there is always someone directly in front of you who has big hair. Lately this phenomenon has come with a twist: increasingly, the big hair in front of you is grey, or even white. The gig-going habit no longer fades at 40 or 50.' That law is now unremarkable, in the same way that people no longer point at women bus drivers and make driving-related remarks, as they used to 25 years ago.

Robin Wight, CEO of ad agency WCRS, describes older people from an advertiser's point of view: They're increasingly likely to have a 'non-ageing mind in an ageing body with a maturing wallet'. Many Groovy Old Men fall headlong into this category. And many more will do so in the future. So, *The Word* magazine boasts an unusual mix of literature, TV, movies and people from all eras alongside the pop. Hence Roy Hattersley rubbing shoulders with Led Zep. Hepworth adds that the mag 'likes to think Bob Dylan, Tom Waits or Richard Thompson exist in the same framework as Charles Dickens, T.S. Eliot or Tony Hancock'. This is a timeless, ageless GOM-friendly formula. More importantly, *The Word* has started to practise frog-safety marketing, defiantly appealing to as wide an audience as it can, all the while studiously avoiding the 'O' word, whereas *Q* etc. repeatedly submit to the boringly tried and tested '100 best' list format, a mainstay for the less adventurous younger reader who watches 100-best digital TV music shows while logged on to Frogbook. I mean Facebook.

I'm indebted to marketing guru Dick Stroud for a lot of this analysis. His view, expressed in a book, *The 50-Plus Market*, aimed at marketing professionals, boils down, like his frog, to some simple GOM-friendly messages.

* The older, wealthier demographic is growing exponentially: the 50–70 age group will grow by 3 million in the next fifteen years; much more than double the growth in 15–34-year-olds in the same period.

*Older people are no longer stuck in their ways; can be easily persuaded to be unfaithful if not promiscuous when it comes to brand loyalty; they currently feel that most advertising ignores them; and have greater life-expectancy, as well as cash.

* This doesn't mean all advertising and PR efforts have to feature well-preserved 60-somethings whose smiles proudly announce a total absence of denture-adhesion problems. Effective marketing to older people means an age-neutral approach when it comes to the vast majority of stuff. Apart from the obvious, often elasticated products.

Sadly, there has, according to Dick Stroud, been little research into more obvious differences in older people – the difference between men and women, for example. Stroud ventures that women, according to common wisdom, have been more confident in their attitude to ageing, and I'd repeat that the reason for this is they've discussed it and reflected upon it more, over a longer period of time and in a diversity of ways, including spending a lot of money on trying to stop it happening so fast and disguising its effects. Stroud quotes extensively from remarks made by those responsible for flogging fruit smoothies, fair trade coffee and mobile phones, all of whom ignore age demographics when it comes to marketing and advertising, and lauds the Guinness advert featuring the old but fit geezer, once an Olympic champ, swimming against a clock which has been timed to pour the perfect pint. You can imagine that this guy then towels himself off, and sits with his pint and the latest copy of *The Word*, to read about Roy Hattersley's taste in music. Well, maybe not.

The company that runs *The Word* once discussed buying *The Oldie*. Which is odd. Because, as discussed, *The Word*, while welcoming hims ancient and modern, never describes anyone as old. Whereas *The Oldie*, unsurprisingly, is explicitly, unrepentantly, grumpily 'O'-rated. A lot of it is well-crafted moaning about the modern world by excellent writers, some of whom seem hell-bent on winning an unadvertised 'reactionary of the month' contest. On a visit to *Oldie* HQ, I ask Richard Ingrams, its creator, whether *The Oldie* has changed at all in this respect, and he starts off rather seriously saying how he believes only in gradual change, but is suddenly overcome by helpless and unexplained giggles. 'It has to change', he says, struggling for breath, '… it has to change because so many of its contributors … *die*!' Ingrams finds this very funny indeed, as if mortality was some crazy function of management, arbitrarily put in place to keep the creative wheels turning.

The trouble with *The Oldie* is that it's fast becoming the house journal for a breed that doesn't exist any more. It's a bit like reading a paper aimed at, I don't know, Vikings or Georgians. Interesting, but after a while, you want it to join the real world. So I've come to *The Oldie* on two missions. To become the magazine's rock critic and to annoy Richard Ingrams by tracing minute particles of Groovy Old Manhood in his flapping corduroy trousers. This may seem like suggesting that I consumer-test some condoms for a report in the *Catholic Herald*, a contraception in terms, so to speak, but no. Because, since its birth in 1992, *The Oldie* has changed a bit. It has a website and a rather good writer about technology called Webster, who cleverly punctures some of the more outlandish claims of nerd PR. *The Oldie* also has one or two regular contributors who may well see out the decade. And occasionally popular culture is treated as if it's not something smelly to be held at arm's length. But it still proudly announces that it has one foot in the grave, suggests people buy it before they snuff it, and generally makes light of death, but heavy weather of old age. Occasionally it's downright nasty, buts mostly it's just a bit crusty.

However, when I arrive with my message that Sir Herbert

Gussett[3] is a member of an endangered species and that older people, especially older men like Ingrams, are likely to change in their outlook, Ingrams recovers from the titters and is eventually pensive, concluding: 'I haven't come to terms with it.' And I suspect he doesn't mean to. 'I very rarely take editorial decisions', he says, which in any other editor might be a worrying admission. Although he has taken one, which is not to have me – or anyone else – as regular rock critic. Even when I suggest that ex-Kink, Ray Davies, whose album *Working Man's Café* was given away free on the front of the *Sunday Times*, may have invented 'grump rock'. I suspect he likes the grump bit, but not the rock bit. He hates pop music. But can someone who hates pop music be a Groovy Old Man? Inspired by finding traces of grooviness in those who initially appear to have none, I try to test a theory that even the grumpiest tweedster – or in Ingrams' case, corduroyal – has imbibed homeopathic traces of hip, merely by dint of living through the relevant part of history.

Ingrams is having none of it and invokes the spirit of Peter Cook, who invented for satirical purposes an imaginary band, modelled on The Beatles: 'It was the only time I can remember when Peter actually wrote a piece – usually he came into the

3 Gussett is a synonym for those retired upper-crust gents who used to write to the *Daily Telegraph*, apoplectic with rage, about something horridly modern. According to Ingrams, these have been purged from the *Telegraph*'s letters pages in order to make the paper look younger. That very week, Gussett and gusset-related matters hit the headlines with grumpy Jeremy Paxman alleging a lack of support in Marks & Spencer's men's underwear.

offices of *Private Eye* and just verbalised. He actually wrote it out ...' Ingrams collapses into giggles again. Cook wrote: 'I want you to meet four very exciting Turds.' The Turds became all-purpose-target pop stars in *Private Eye* in the same way that Sir Herbert Gussett became a byword for apoplectic retired colonels.

Ingrams now warms to his task of explaining why he thinks pop is crap and why it can't be a regular part of *The Oldie*. (He refuses to have a bridge column or a jazz column in his paper for similarly personal reasons. He finds both boring.) The anti-pop reason is that when he sits down to play the piano for a sing-song he finds that, whereas people can all sing along to selections from (his choice) *My Fair Lady*, they can't as easily join in with a Beatles song. I don't – though tempted – point out that perhaps the lack of joining-in has more to do with the Ingrams piano style than the comparative merits of Lerner and Loewe and Lennon and McCartney. Just as I don't point out that Peter Cook took the mick out of The Beatles as a clever and conscious act of genius-baiting, an example of Cook's and the early *Eye*'s consistent approach to satire. Satirise everything that everyone else is eulogising.

Initially I conclude that Ingrams has no GOM content at all. *The Oldie* is a brilliant idiosyncratic magazine based on a brilliant but uncompromisingly idiosyncratic old man, but eccentricity doesn't equate to grooviness and there's an end to it. As for *The Oldie*, it might become a guilty pleasure for Groovy Old Men, if only for the brilliant cartoons, but no more. It has been an entertaining but wasted visit. Except that as we chit-chat our way to the end of the conversation, Ingrams lets slip that the following evening he will be dining with Tariq Ali. Despite the dramatic differences in almost all aspects of their lives, apart from both being men of a certain age, they enjoy each other's company. Like Ali, Ingrams has been consistently faithful to his teenage roots. While schoolmates and co-*Private Eye* men Willie Rushton and Christopher Booker played in the school jazz band (Ingrams has consistently hated jazz), Ingrams has had no pop music moment. His only joy has been pomp-puncturing, whether it's of the beaks at school, The Beatles, Blair or Brown. He is friends with the Archbishop of Canterbury and Tariq Ali. He is satire's own Tommy Steele, but in much looser trousers. I conclude significant GOM quotient in Ingrams, and while I hope this annoys him, I suspect that it won't. Groovy Old Men are unflappable.

They have made a modest entry into *Saga* magazine under the editorship of Emma Soames, who used to be Ingrams' deputy at *The Oldie*. Before her arrival, '*Saga* magazine seemed to be talking to a pre-war generation', she explains, and it was her job to modernise. She was appointed with the express intention of rock 'n' rolling the magazine up, hence the inclu-sion of Mark Ellen, Seasick Steve and judiciously chosen album reviews (Alison Moyet, Georgie Fame, Springsteen, Radiohead). In fact, *Saga* is the only magazine I know to have full-frontal 'O'-rated content *and* rock 'n' roll coverage. But *Saga* still has the feel of a mid-market woman's title and the advertising to match. 'The fact is, more women buy *Saga* than men, and the advertising reflects that. But I do try and get at least one thing in for men every month.' The trouble is, the demographic, based on marketing insurance to the less risky but increasingly frisky over 50s, is very wide. Fifty to eighty and over is a big time span, and the man who's interested in a feature about, say, Bruce Springsteen is less likely to be interested in a feature about a World War Two escape. Unless, of course he's a Groovy Old Man, in which case his interests might span both. But first-generation GOMs are, as discussed, thin on the ground. And none that I know reads *Saga*. The Saga brand emphasises the idea of a homogenous older community who meet, network and share holidays. They love each other's company. This seems to be the lifestyle projected in the magazine. So much so that Ms Soames has been keen to track one story for *Saga* mag about a special old-age micro-community of which she has heard. With house prices soaring, family life fracturing and pensions dwindling, half a dozen or so oldies decide to buy a house and move in together. Their pooled resources and shared outlook make it a brilliant and autonomous alternative to the nursing home. They're the new kind of old people, they exercise, take care about what they eat, and one assumes the mix is leavened by Groovy Old Men and women who have heated conversations with the *Saga* louts, all the while playing Scrabble and exchanging tips about wide-fitting shoes and arguing about what to put on the sound system. 'Gimme Shelter' meets gimme sheltered accommodation.

There's only one problem with the story. It's fiction. 'We've looked high and low for a real example, but it's an urban myth', moans Ms Soames. It does conjure up images of The Young Ones, reassembled to become The Old Ones, with Rik

Mayall, Ade Edmondson and Nigel Planer back together and still arguing about Cliff, who seems not to have aged at all in his predictable cameo appearance. In fact this isn't as far-fetched as it might seem. Edmondson has already joined the Bonzo Dog Doo-Dah Band. GOM band of choice.

In the real world, people and their choice of reading and viewing and listening is much more arbitrary than media people would like to think. Groovy Old Men are just as likely to settle down with a copy of the *Financial Times*, *The Lady*, *Beano* or *Hefty Throbbers*. But with the grey pound in the ascendant, the money people behind *The Oldie*, *Saga*, *The Word* and others see future Groovy Old Men as a target. Somewhere in Britain an enterprising media lecturer has set the brief to his advertising students to create a Groovy Old Stairlift. Hitherto, advertised stairlift passengers have all been of the Thora Hird variety, or direct descendants thereof. The new image will feature a greying big-haired guy with a guitar or a laptop and a joke about 'Stairlift to Heaven'. But try as they might, the mags – if not the media as a whole – will never get a handle on current old men, Groovy or not. Because they're not easy marks in terms of marketing.

However, the internet already has got a handle. At its mention, Richard Ingrams gets the giggles again at the idea of his ancient readers locked onto their laptops. 'Oh, they're all into the internet … because they haven't got anything else to do!' What they will be able to do, more and more, is shape their own media, sampling online from *The Word*, *The Oldie*, *Saga*, the BBC, *Hefty Throbbers* or equiv. For once, the consumer is moving faster than the supplier, and in some cases designing the supply. A self-designed home page with lots of links to the bits of magazines, newspapers, radio and TV downloads, podcasts and social networking that suit them.

The internet is the last chapter of technological history in the current GOM timeline, the one that started with the end of the 78 record and the start of the 45rpm single.[4] In the case of our Groovy Old Men, since the age of sixteen they have not only been a music fancier and possibly player, but also a student of 50 years of changing means of delivery: 78rpm, 45rpm, EP, LP, stereo, transistor, 8-track, cassette, CD. Like Duncan Sandys and his brand-new Polaroid, the stuff is sometimes more important than the content.

So, while the internet can be used passively to browse *The Oldie*'s holiday offers, gardening tips or elasticated products, Groovy Old Men are still using it actively and profitably. Here's Dave, nearing 60, retired engineer, lives in the country, loves wildlife and photography, big music buff, plays bass, pedal steel guitar, but can't play live any more with the same band he's been with since the seventies. Instead, he helps make his favoured Americana-type music online, recording his contributions on piano, guitar, mandolin or pedal steel, then sending them online for the rest of the band to mix electronically.

Richard, aged 60, is still a bee farmer, but he's now also an internet service provider, though not on the scale of BT. Until

---

4 The 45 vinyl single eclipsed the breakable 78 record in 1958 in the UK; GOMs were in their teens.

2004, the 1,200 population of his Worcestershire village couldn't get very good broadband. Now, thanks to his intervention, they can have a high-speed broadband connection using wireless technology. It's run as a not-for-profit community-based outfit. Part of his inspiration is being old enough to remember when electricity was first piped to a rural community's most distant members, and the different uses they were able to find for it. He has diverse users on the network: some farmers like himself, others from the ranks of the middle-class retired. These include a tapestry-maker and a Groovy-sounding guy who uses the connection to get old motor cycle parts from eBay. We can come to ancient bikers in a minute, but staying with Richard, here's an example of a man who transcends the traditional image of the silver surfer. The SS has learnt, admirably late in life, all about computers by collecting step-by-step part-work magazines especially designed for the older learner. Richard, meanwhile, has been a farmer all his life, and has also been fiddling with computers since the seventies, and even won a competition for a computerised braille/speech converter.

Peter Jenner, the original manager of Pink Floyd, still managing bands in his early 60s, is also an online activist, spending a lot of time campaigning with record industry executives and government ministers for a new kind of digital marketplace for pop. There has never been a better time for older people to be getting music. The famed breakdown of the traditional marketplace, for so long dominated by big record companies, can only benefit them. They can get what they want, old or new, when they want it, irrespective of what the big shops have in stock, the big mags say is good, or the big record companies plug for radio play. Richard Ingrams: 'Yes, but do people really want …' – and here he pauses to decide which outré band he will use as a synonym for redundant rock – '… do people really want *The Shadows*?'

The answer is 'probably', and not only The Shadows; they may also want Shostakovich, The Slits and other mixed musical names specially selected to test denture-diction. And why shouldn't they have it at a time when rock bands are giving away music online and Ray Davies just released his grump rock album for free on the front of a Sunday newspaper? Old rockers are storming out of their record companies in a huff and storming back to the concert stage, you don't have to queue for gig tickets any more, you can get more or less anything musical illegally for free, Michael Caine's a pop star and Amy Winehouse is the new Dusty Springfield, only more tragic. Jenner's concern is that while the Wild West atmosphere prevails, the artists are the ones in danger of getting heard but not paid. His idea is based on 50 years of understanding of the music business. In Peter's childhood, his vicar father palled up with a congregant who was a big noise in the local west London record factory. He later became the connection for the supply of jazz records Jenner couldn't hear anywhere else.

Jenner's idea is simply that internet service providers become the conduit for paying for all music. When you get a broadband account, a proportion of the fee goes straight into a fund, out of which music artists will be paid per download. The middle men – the record companies who allegedly inflate the price of music – will be truly cut out. Shostakovich, The Slits and The Shadows et al. will benefit according to how many times people have listened to 'The Rise and Fall of Flingl Bunt', etc. Internet service providers have quietly benefited from the popularity of illegal music downloads (as they have from other unwholesome online activity), then innocently thrown up their hands and said: 'We just provide the pipe, what people feed in or suck out is nothing to do with us.' Now they can be part of the legal process. It's a licence fee, very much like the BBC licence fee, and it'll make illegal downloading as redundant as the BBC made pirate radio by launching Radio 1. It'll have widespread frog-friendly appeal and the guys will be able to download Bat for Lashes *and* Big Bill Broonzy. And an old bloke thought it up.

Nothing surprising about that, of course. The fact that there are creative, clever people in their 60s still working for something in which they believe should be unremarkable. This applies to women as much as to men, but I wonder whether Groovy Old Manhood will come too easily to future generations whose hinterlands aren't so diverse. Something to be owned rather than won. I've noticed, looking back through the interviews for this book, that often, describing a car, a musical instrument, a camera, a significant purchase of any kind, the circumstances of the purchase and the price paid are recalled with vivid detail. Men can be fetishist about certain of their purchases, and I can't help imagining Duncan Sandys, the man largely responsible for the end of National Service, taking an undue interest in his Polaroid camera – the only one in Britain, don't forget – rather than the activity he was depicting in chapter two.

It may be for the older men that those first guitars, records, cameras were all the more prized because they cost a lot at a time of great austerity. Whereas the *next* generation of potential Groovy Old Men can simply buy their way back into their histories and teenage desires. In 2008, insurance companies noted that while motorcycle accident fatalities have decreased among the under-30s, they doubled for over-50s in a ten-year period because of the fashion for older men to buy powerful bikes. They passed their tests on mopeds, then switched to cars, and back on the saddle – this time of a 1,000cc bike – they're a danger to themselves. Compare and contrast with the guys who never stopped riding and spot the Groovy.

In a way, the same can be said of the other male icon, the guitar. There's now a vigorous trade in vintage guitars, especially American electric guitars made in the fifties. They were expensive enough in their heyday in Britain, but now, mainly because of their rarity value, they can be worth hundreds of thousands of pounds, and there are plenty of men in their 50s who are happy to spend large amounts, while comforting themselves that what they're buying is an investment. I have to confess a certain interest here, as I have covered this trade as a journalist, writing the odd magazine or newspaper article about the dangers of forgery and the inflated prices of guitars that claim to be previously owned by Jimi Hendrix. One dealer who has done very well from this trade has a nickname for wealthy older men with a Fender-fetish and a thick cash wad: 'Dentists'. The name may be a bit dentist-ist, but you can see the point. The image is of a man who has spent years peering into people's cake-holes and latterly feels he's earned himself a slice of the cake. So he buys himself an authentic beaten-up but valuable Strat and a ticket to ride back to 1971. The fact that the Strat looks the worse for wear makes it even better. Because so does the dentist. Dealers will tell you that the worst thing you can do to a classic early-sixties American-built instrument is try to restore it to its birthday beauty. While the dentist, metaphorically, has spent 30 years in sterile surroundings and an immaculate white coat, the Strat has been living a rock 'n' roll lifestyle, and looks it. And is still an investment. And I apologise to any dentist in his late 50s reading this who has spent all his days with a drill in his hand and all his evenings with a plectrum.

However, lifestyle changes make the new batch of Groovy Old Men, those in their late 50s awaiting grooviness, much harder to categorise. They lack the historical credentials. The music-based rebellions they conducted or observed are mere reverberations of the rebellions that took place during the teenage years of the original groovies in the fifties. The new generation accept a consumerist youth culture as the status quo. In fact, for them the very words 'status quo' conjure up 'Pictures of Matchstick Men' before anything else. Like today's young teenagers who don't remember a pre-internet world, the boomers scarcely remember what life was like before The

Beatles. They own big CD collections, but less big history connections. One difficult-to-categorise group, for whom a kind of ownership on a larger scale is paramount, might be referred to as The Great, the Good and the Groovy.

It's a problematic combination. There are virtually no significant examples of The Great, the Good and the Groovy in the first generation of Groovy Old Men, possibly because those who anoint the Great and the Good are innately anti-Groovy. We have already considered the case of Baron Triesman of Tottenham. Once a dashing radical who led a daring protest against a real baddie, he's now a loyal member of New Labour and a former (unelected) government minister. He has a vigorous and youthful outlook. But I have already agreed not to classify him as Groovy or otherwise because of family ties. I hinted at another reason. Recently he left the front benches of the House of Lords and became Chairman of the Football Association. If I ruled him Groovy I would come under immediate suspicion for nepotism. This is a man with enviable ticket-access. Best if he's left unclassified.[5]

Elsewhere among the ranks of Great, Good and Groovy, I also have problems of classification. Among them are men who start life pretty Groovy, but are then seduced by Greatness, which they think is Good. I discuss this with Emma Soames, who spots the problem: 'You mean there are so many people looking Groovy on the outside as opposed to Groovy through

---

5 Obviously, David, if you do have access to any spares, try to avoid dates where Charlton Athletic have home matches. Thanks.

and through.' This is right. Good point. If grooviness is in the eye of the beholder, and the beholder is female, and money/power is part of the attraction, we must rethink. 'Cool old dudes', Emma muses, scanning the London penthouse hotel bar where we're having tea, as if one might materialise any minute. One doesn't.

We settle on Richard Branson as a test case. One of a good deal of men in their 50s and older whose success, as she puts it, 'has been based around something associated with youth'. Emma is particularly pleased, having previously secured an interview with Branson for *Saga* – a perfect cover-boy for a magazine that wants Groovy Old Men to read it. Branson: public schoolboy, dyslexic,[6] young sports fiend, creative entrepreneur whose failed teenage businesses included sales of Christmas trees and budgerigars, who founded a magazine for students and then challenged the record retail business on its own overfed turf. A famously tieless man with a big grin and two airline hostesses or a balloon or a mountain in every publicity picture. But inside, I suggest to Emma, is a man in a pinstripe suit. Emma, less prejudiced perhaps than I am about such things, says that Groovy Old Men's grooviness is based on the fact that they can do 'pinstripey things' and still

6 In an as-yet unpublished article for the education press entitled 'Hooray for Dyslexia', I outline the benefits of the condition, which is over-represented in Groovy Old Men. The effect – in the first generation at least – is to make them even more determined to kick against the pricks and succeed in their own terms.

be a bit Groovy as well. By which I guess she means wield power.

I try to think of some other GG&G egs. Alan Yentob, BBC lifer, a man who helped invent a new type of TV arts documentary of the kind I adore, before becoming a very senior BBC figure. A genuine creative, committed to proper public service TV, who later starts to present his own strand of arts documentaries, apparently for the same reason that a dog licks its own balls. Because he can. Another problematic candidate is Lord Saatchi. Long-term collector and rock fan. Changed politics using advertising as a tool, possibly not for the better. Changed the face of advertising with brilliant campaigns like the one for the Health Education Council, promoting contraception and featuring the image of a pregnant man. As an art collector, started a new and lucrative kind of art, mainly by buying it and inflating its price, if not its worth. Second wife Kay Hartenstein characterised him as 'a man of crushes – cars, clothes, artists'. Damien Hirst has called him a 'shopaholic', Saatchi has described himself as 'a gorger of the briefly new', according to the BBC website. No question, Saatchi's partner Nigella Lawson would describe Saatchi as a Groovy Old Man. But his consumerist tendencies might worry some. Fifty-Quid Bloke is one thing. Fifty-Thousand-Quid Bloke may be quite another.

Another problematic example is Alan Johnson, government minister, a rare one who didn't need a team of advisors to help him choose his Desert Island Discs. (The radio desert island is a great place to spot them, by the way, as is any street market, cinema queue, art gallery, some sea fronts, and places where kites are flown.) He has publicly cast aspersions on Tony Blair's guitar playing and is himself a former member of a band – the In Betweens, a multi-ethnic band with a girl singer. He's also a former shelf-stacker and postman, who 'sort of' dropped out of school at fifteen to get into music. And although he dropped music and took up trade unionism and then politics, it's his son who is a professional musician and successful recording engineer. And Alan wears a tie. So Groovy on the inside. Pinstripey on the outside.

In fact, the sole Great, Good and Groovy Old Man I can unequivocally hand the order of the GOM has already got a gong – Sir Paul Smith. I fall back on my excuse of never having met Saatchi, Yentob, Branson or Johnson, so I don't have to issue a rating. I get the impression from Smith that his has been a labour of love rather than ambition, and that, sure, he's an astute businessman who likes things (though he swapped his Porsche for a clapped-out BMW and a Mini) and he enjoys his wealth. He has a second Mini for his house in Italy. And he, paradoxically, has improved the lifestyle of many a Groovy Old Man, present and future.

But diversification of lifestyle, or to put it back in its protective punctuation, 'lifestyle', is going to make future Groovy Old Man-spotting more complicated. It may be easier to look like one, and own the trappings of one, and those trappings may range from an iPod to a multi-million-pound corporation. But that ease of looking like one will make it harder to be one. Hunger for power, money and things doesn't seem very Groovy to me. Modesty has to be an ingredient, and passion, possibly. Perhaps I've spent too long with first-generation blokes who don't seem to care so much about being Great and Good. Or Groovy for that matter.

CHAPTER SEVEN

The Future's So Bright

'The Future's So Bright, I Gotta Wear Shades'
Timbuk3

I'm in the garden with … well, it doesn't matter who. We've been talking for a long time so we've come outside for a break and he suddenly looks at me, a kind of panic flickering briefly behind his eyes. '*Who* did you say you were?' I remind him about my mission and immediately he looks relieved. A bit sheepish, too.

This isn't about eternal life. Groovy Old Men aren't immune to decrepitude. In fact a lot of these guys are more gloomy about the future after they've gone than about the ravages of their own old age. And go they will. I have a dread, given the subject matter, that one will go between completion of the text of this book and publication. So for the most part I've kept away, when talking to the men, from the subject of the darker side of old age and death in particular. If they've brought it up, fine.

There's optimism as well, in joyful amounts, long-term and

short-term. John Harris, born 1945, is a terrific example. He has a deep, out-of-season tan when we meet, a carefully trimmed beard, chooses what you might call 'backpacker chic' – thick-looking chinos, expensive-looking fleece, deep blue shirt, good wide smile. Although on the young side (his birth date is close to the boom cut-off), his CV is perfect. Told he was stupid at school, twice an eleven-plus failure, the sudden and close death of both his parents fuels his anger. He loses God instantly, becomes an anti-nuclear weapons activist, gets shunted around the family as an orphan teenager, is banned from taking A-levels, ends up living in a bedsit, working as an articled clerk in a solicitors' office in the West End of London. He starts to educate himself – art galleries, the newly opened National Theatre and reading. CND leads him to Bertrand Russell. Russell's anti-nuclear work *Has Man a Future?* leads John to his *History of Western Philosophy*. He manages, through a mixture of assertiveness and cheek, to get a place at university, despite lack of credentials. Because of lack of credentials, possibly.

All this leads him to his comfortable office at the University of Manchester, where he's one of Britain's most successful philosophers. Sure, this sounds like the cue for either a Monty Python sketch about a very successful philosopher (played by Michael Palin[1] in a nice suit, probably) or an examination question: 'What constitutes success in the study of philos-

---

[1] *Saga*-acceptable GOM.

ophy?' I just pasted that question into Google, and spent a happy hour in quotation land. Aristotle on happiness is particularly good.

For John Harris,[2] successful philosopher, happiness is driving across Europe in his four-wheel drive vehicle to the family holiday house near Florence. He needs the four-wheel drive in Italy because the house is set in rough terrain. It's non-stop Bob Dylan, all the way. He has the complete works and he flips from classic to new with joyful abandon. Harris loves Dylan. John's wife, meanwhile, flies over to the house. Good arrangement.

Harris believes in enhancement. He says we do not die of old age but the diseases of old age. He thinks we can and should systematically prevent these diseases and many others using stem-cell therapy and other genetic interventions. Humanity can be remodelled. His book, *Enhancing Evolution*, explains why he believes this. It's controversial and occasionally difficult stuff, mainly because those who oppose his view have a horror of messing with the building blocks of humanity. Genetic re-engineering. In putting what he calls the 'ethical case for making better people', Harris destroys the distinction between therapy and enhancement. Nobody doubts the ethical case for vaccination. But the far-reaching enhancements that Harris is talking about are, he argues, philosophically indis-

2 Harris is the Sir David Alliance Professor of Bioethics at the University of Manchester School of Law, joint editor of the *Journal of Medical Ethics* and a member of the UK Human Genetics Commission.

tinguishable from vaccination, which is simply enhancing the immune system to fight disease more effectively. And in Harris's perspective this *is* about eternal life. Or even immortality. Or at least a new kind of human. If the diseases of old age can be eradicated in some, and if tissue regeneration can be achieved, we're talking life spans in thousands of years, and a new, more sophisticated type of human, man and woman.

But, from my (selfish) point of view, what will these changes do to the sales of Bob Dylan albums? Does it mean that Groovy Old Manhood will become the norm, the Ted and the Dudley? There may well be an ugly division between the enhanced and the non-enhanced. Groovy Old Supermen and Superwomen and just Groovy Old Men and Women. Unfair though that may seem, it's no different to the gap between people because of currently different levels of medical treat-ment or social care: the gap between people who want to, and have access to, and can afford to choose to pay for enhance-ment, and the others who can't or don't want to. The super-old may well, he thinks, gain that status as a result of treatments decided upon by their parents at their birth or in the womb. In this respect, Harris's super-old may be different to Groovy-old. Groovy-old got there because of their choices. Super-old, if enhanced during their childhood, had none. Not that they should complain. 'What would the child who was left unen-hanced say to their parents about that?' asks Harris. The vacci-nation parallel is a powerful one.

Enhancement doesn't stop at biological efficiency. The capacity for enjoyment can be enhanced as well, says Harris: 'I do have the attitudes characteristic of my particular epoch – that pleasure isn't sinful … human enhancement is about all of the things you want to enhance … health, intelligence and insight and all of those things conduce to pleasure. Pleasure should be available indefinitely and enhancement technologies will make those pleasures safer: alcohol without the danger of addiction or liver damage. If we can make either ourselves or things we consume safer, to avoid bad effects, that would be great.' The enhanced are likely to be more beautiful, mainly because, as Harris puts it, 'Insofar as we take pleasure in beauty and value it, it makes sense to enhance genetically for beauty.' And as there isn't just one way to be beautiful, Groovy Old People will be beautifully diverse. The trouble is they won't be old. The conventional distinctions of chronological age will be far less valid.

I lob what now seems a weedy ball at the Harris wicket. The prospect of death, as experienced by the old, gives them a valuable perspective on the finite nature of life. Nearness to the end can result in sharper focus about the whole of life. Old is good. We need old. Nope. Harris says everything has to be on the basis of evidence and argument, and 'The old don't have a monopoly of evidence and argument.'

Other than adding the profile of Harris, a brilliant and stimulating Groovy Old Man from the younger end of the age range, I'm not initially sure what I've gained in practice from our discussion. Except perhaps that I can add to my list of fictional specimens (Alfie, Billy Liar, Howard Kirk) an extra though slightly anomalous name. Doctor Who. Probably as played by Christopher Eccleston for the sex appeal or Tom Baker for the period authenticity. As Groovy as you can get (why else do kids still adore him?) and as old as the hills. That's not to demote Professor Harris's views to the status of a Saturday tea-time entertainment. And the reason for talking about all this now, long before we'll see the result in terms of 4,000-year-old Dylan fans (apart from the very good reason that it's interesting) is practical. We're at the beginning of understanding the techniques that will bring about these changes, and we need to debate the ethical problems that relate to them, before deciding on the benefits of a Groovy old life and a long-enhanced one.

Professor Sube Banerjee[3] brings only cautious optimism. He's a long-term Clash fan, listener to weird New York radio stations, and consultant psychiatrist specialising in work with older people. Despite his heavy metal hairstyle and musical tastes, at 45 he's far too young to be considered for GOM status. But not too young to have an internationally respected expert view of ageing, especially dementia. And dementia is on the rise, as life expectancy increases. The older population will grow in numbers, and dementia will grow with it: 700,000 people experience dementia now – in 30 years that will double. Life expectancy among the over-65s is growing[4] for both men

3 Clinical Director of Old Age Psychiatry and Professor of Mental Health and Ageing at King's College London.
4 Life expectancy at age 65 in the UK has reached its highest level ever for both men and women. Men aged 65 could expect to live a further 16.9 years and women a further 19.7 years if mortality rates remained the same as they were in 2004–06 (Office for National Statistics).

and women, with women living longer, and there are no real signs that men will catch women up, for the moment. We still have the legacy of different types of work and health patterns to contend with. A smoking miner active in the 1980s miners' strike has a statistically greater chance of an earlier death than a non-smoking dinner lady from the same mining village, to put it crudely. There may even be some lasting biological factors to do with the way women's sex hormones protected them in childbearing years, which mean they have a chance of a longer life. However, smoking striking miners and the like are a dying breed for historical as well as medical reasons. Soon us softies, who will be in the majority, will be coming to the end of non-smoking white-collar jobs and will be collecting our still-adequate pensions and heading for the hills. Or the shops.

For the meantime, though, grooviness might increase quality of life for men, but it won't increase longevity. And long-term recreational drug use is likely to kill or harm you early. 'You're messing with neurotransmitters here!' warns Professor Banerjee, urgently. 'Moving them about, using them up, blocking them, changing them!' Soon, in as little as fifteen years, the drugs of choice (apart from Viagra and echinacea and statins) will be aimed at halting or slowing down dementia. Banerjee warns they'll be more expensive, initially dangerous and they won't be a cure.

Almost everything we've said about the science of ageing applies equally to women and men. For example, 678 elderly nuns in a Catholic institution in the United States were the subject of some interesting research into the effects of ageing. Uncomplicated by sex and drugs and drink and probably rock 'n' roll, the shared background of these women made them an excellent subject for study. The fact that they were nuns rather than monks is irrelevant. What was learned from them by epidemiologist Professor David A. Snowdon, PhD, is likely to be applicable to either sex. He was given access to the early writing of these women, and he extrapolated that those who had greater linguistic ability in early life were less likely to develop dementia, whereas low linguistic ability was associated with dementia and shorter lifespan. And those who showed positive emotions in early life live longer. These findings appear to help with my theory of Groovy Old Men, all of whom have excellent linguistic ability (I've got a heap of tapes to prove it) and most of whom had positive emotions when young. But they apply to both sexes.

The only factor that Professor Banerjee suggests that applies especially to Groovy Old Men, as a theory rather than as a proven fact, is to do with 'coarsening' of existing personality in dementia. Talking of older people in the tones of a man sticking his neck out, he explains: 'Women are by and large *nicer* than men ... The life that men lived in the past developed in them a sort of toughness.' In other words grumpy old men get grumpier in dementia. So do Groovy Old Men get groovier? Groovy Old Men are, of course, very pleasant and always have been. Many in the

first batch are men of the first generation where that toughness hasn't always been bred in the bone. Which does lead
towards the idea of Groovy Old Male Alzheimer's patients.
It's not as bad as it sounds. The late George Melly, the writer
and jazz singer, was a terrific example. 'The great thing about
Alzheimer's', he is reported to have joked, 'is you meet such
nice new people!'

It may well be that this is a golden age for Groovy Old
Men. The first is certainly a golden generation, and the generations that follow immediately will have a lot of benefits.
Salary-related pensions, early retirement, better health – all
play their part in making a Groovy life groovier. It's likely that
men will stop paying the high cost of living associated, in
previous generations, with war, work and stress. They'll be
less likely to shout 'Turn that noise down!' and more likely
to ask what that noise is, then download it. Culturally, the
back catalogue of the last 60 years, all of it available online,
can't be bettered.

Technology will probably continue to improve Groovy Old
Men's lives. However, this may be a short-lived golden technological age. Internet technologies offer great freedoms. Older
people will feel more in touch, less isolated. And it's still more
or less the Wild West out there. However, there are increasing
signs that intense commerce will fight its way back into technology. Your social networking site will start to look more
like an advertising hoarding, based on its knowledge of your
purchasing and browsing habits and those of your friends.

This is happening already. Go back to your computers and prepare to advertise cruises.[5]

In a way, the idea of cruises might be doubly relevant. Noah might have been a Groovy Old Man, and the waters are rising again. One feature of a lot of Groovy Old Men is concern for the long-term future. Andrew Kerr, Glastonbury original, proudly points to his early green credentials. He organised the world's first organic agricultural show, from which Radio 4's *Costing the Earth* programme was broadcast by wind power. The company behind the agricultural show didn't make any money, so he went to be a gardener in Oxfordshire, which he liked. He also applied for the job of head gardener at Highgrove. It called for all sorts of scientific knowledge and he just told them that he knew 'an awful lot about compost'. Renewal is his thing. He didn't get the job, which is a pity, because I get the impression he and Prince Charles would have got on. (Prince Charles: Groovy Old King? Discuss.) Mike Bell, the man from the Portobello Gold, the pub full of Groovy Old Men, is looking for a property 'above the waterline' for his young children. One guy I won't name is planning to adopt. Older men with very small

5 During the writing of this book, Facebook founder Mark Zuckerberg apologised to users for exploiting their browsing habits for the purposes of advertising. Meanwhile, internet service providers have been experimenting with secretly watching the browsing habits of users so that they can 'deliver the right ad to the right person at the right time'. Baby boomers – who expect to be marketing targets – will be less affronted by the internet invasion of advertisers than original Groovy Old Men.

children is a trend that will continue. Does having children help make you Groovy in old age? Very possibly. Whether it's 'fair' or not to have children late in life is a bit off my brief, because it's a decision shared between man and woman. And anyone, man or woman, who decides to have a child to prolong their own feelings of youth is destined for disaster. All the same, if I were a small child with an old dad, I know what kind I'd prefer.

CHAPTER EIGHT

Three Funerals. No Weddings

I'm dappled and drowsy and ready to sleep ...
Simon and Garfunkel,
'52nd Street Bridge Song (Feeling Groovy)'

The police were a bit hysterical, by the sound of it. They were screaming 'Put your hands in the air and don't touch the sword!' It was plain for anyone to see that the sword, though genuine, was for ceremony only. It was still in its scabbard, for a start. And the man carrying it, albeit a bit 'alternative'-looking, was leading a procession through the streets of north-west London. Behind him, the hearse bearing the earthly remains of Kenneth Sams, 81, a sure and certain candidate for the title Groovy Old Man. In fact, even better, GOM with the Wind, as Ken's first love was flying kites.

The story comes courtesy of Kenneth's son, Greg Sams, who told it to me in the year he faces his 60th birthday. And in a way it returns us to the first story in the book, about fathers and sons. My friend Steve's dad, as seen in the pub. If we want to look at the conditions that create the next generation, then this much is certain. Groovy Old Men will beget Groovy Old Men. Steve, mid-40s, is as much a certainty as Greg, 59, when we spoke. Greg's dad's funeral in 2003 was appropriately unusual. First the farcical contretemps with the sword, which Greg says Ken would have enjoyed; a wild party in suburbia with Ken's coffin open for the paying of respects; an early-morning minibus ride to some woodland burial ground in Kent, and finally a humanist interment ceremony with ceremonial bells and sword used.

Greg and Ken rarely rowed. Ken was a relaxed role model who told his son he'd rather he smoked marijuana and drank beer than smoked tobacco and drank Coke. But there was more to Ken than standard hippy. Born 1922 in Bridgeville, Pennsylvania of Syrian immigrant parents, he fought in the Second World War in the Far East and got a Master's degree in English from UCLA thanks to the GI Bill. He subsidised his income in the late forties by selling a special kind of rotary kite on the beach at Santa Monica. The kite was mysterious because nobody could explain exactly how it flew.

Ken was no stranger to mystery. In the early fifties, he came to live in the UK, having got a job as a civilian historian to the United States Air Force to analyse the growing NATO from a US military perspective. He'd also taught himself Arabic and broadcast to Syria on the BBC World Service. In the early sixties, his job took him to Vietnam, where his task was to analyse the escalating war. But Ken, officially entitled Chief of the Air Force Contemporary Historical Evaluator of Combat Operations, ended up partying in Saigon with a solid soundtrack of psychedelic hits sent out from Kensal Rise by teenage son Greg. Mysteriously, the US authorities tolerated their historical evaluator starting a forces magazine called *Grunt*. It was a home-grown alternative to *Stars and Stripes*, the official forces paper, and was produced with unofficial *Stars and Stripes* labour, and it openly solicited anti-military contributions from servicemen. Its circulation was reported to have been 50,000 at its height, with black humour, nudes and cartoons reminiscent of the burgeoning alternative press in the US and the UK. Sams claimed his magazine was the subject of intelligence spying. According to one report, his 'live-in maid' was 'seduced' by a double agent. Sams confessed to young Greg that the maid was his long-term mistress, and was probably an agent for the Vietcong. Others suspected that Sams himself was a CIA plant, a willing double agent whose magazine would be a lightning rod, conducting a steady stream of dissenters into public view. Who knows? Maybe he played both ways. Suffice it to say, he lived in interesting times. Which is, I have to conclude, the most significant factor in a Groovy Old Man's life.

Back in the UK, Ken Sams wasn't the normal kind of dad you'd have as a teenager growing up in suburban north London. Ken's love of kite flying, which he started in the forties, continued well into the nineties. In 1992 a widely reported UFO scare in London was attributed to a Ken Sams kite. He was a fixture on London bridges, flying all sorts of 'UFO' kites (Unconventional Flying Objects) which dazzled and often confused onlookers. Ken's legacy is indirectly to be experienced by the nation in increased UK peanut butter quality. After the Second World War, Ken had a mysterious illness cured by a Japanese doctor, who prescribed what we'd now call a wholefood diet. This became the norm for the Sams family in the forties and fifties. Greg grew up on a diet based on home-baked wholemeal bread. In Britain, Greg at nineteen opened the first UK wholefood restaurant, pioneered the vegeburger, and founded the famous Whole Earth Foods brand, whose peanut butter triumphed with its non-mysterious recipe of being made of one ingredient. Peanuts.

Greg – writer, philosopher, activist, alternative businessman – was always mystified by his teenage schoolmates' reports of rows with parents. 'The only time I was annoyed with my dad was when he dipped into my stash without asking', he recalls. For me, Greg is a perfect example of a second-generation Groovy Old Man, who awaits his 60th birthday very philosophically. Gone is the discontinuity between fathers and sons experienced by the first generation. Greg – and I have to assume others like him – follows naturally in his father's footsteps. That's not to say that you'll certainly be a Groovy Old Man if your dad was. I've seen lots of sons of perfect specimens rebel by reaching, metaphorically and in reality, for suit and tie and traditional values and salaried jobs. But if your dad is or was one, you're more likely to be one. And anti-dad rebellion isn't as prevalent as it was.

I have had the disposal of Andrew Kerr's earthly remains on my mind for months, mainly because of one image. It's his body being prepared for composting. He is the groundsman, gardener, minicab driver, historian, sailor, farmer, housepainter, TV researcher and festival starter, born in 1933, and you may remember he wants his body to go on giving pleasure to others after he dies. He took part in a TV programme where he demonstrated his support for the controversial notion of composting of human remains. Some might find the details grisly, involving as they do disembowelment. But the end result would be a compost that 'could then be incorporated into the family memorial garden. This would be far better than burial, which is too deep for aerobic processes and the wasteful incineration which is damaging to the environment.'

By Andrew's account, the demonstration of human composting for TV was pretty farcical. It would have been difficult to show the process graphically. A rabbit had to take the place of a human. Andrew had suggested a cat, but this was regarded as inappropriate for TV. Andrew lined up some roadkill rabbits and fed one through his beloved green waste shredder. However, he dropped the first rabbit in too quickly, before the camera was ready, and he had to fish it out again. Then, because the rabbits had been hanging about in the back of his car for days and, as he puts it, 'everything had gone solid', no gooily shredded rabbit appeared at the other end. Andrew suggested the addition of some beetroot. This worked a treat. In fact it worked too well, and what issued colourfully forth from the shredder was regarded as not right for 8pm TV. However, the sequence does contain – and it flashes by very fast – an image of a human body, presumably meant to represent Andrew's, in the form of fruit and vegetables.

And the body is disturbingly rolled into what looks like a great big mincer. I phone up Andrew and he supplies the detail. Melon for a head, parsnip tops for eyes. Celery, tomato, plums, and a courgette for the willy. The idea was to make a fruit and veg simulacrum of the not-yet-late Andrew Kerr and feed it into the industrial composter in west London. Sounds harmless. They took enormous pains making the vege-model and shooting it as it went into the machine, then used only a few seconds of the result.

Perhaps it's the speed with which this image goes by that makes it seem macabre. You don't have time to register that the body is made up of fruit and veg until after it has been consumed by the machine. Only then do you realise what you were seeing was essentially the manufacture of a smoothie. Or rather a compostie. But it all comes as a bit of a shock, mainly because of the apparent hunger of the death-mincer. And it's not meant to. 'It's to do with a respect for human life and death and it's rather a beautiful thing', says Andrew. I ask him whether he's got it all organised, the recycling of his real remains. 'Trouble is, it'll cost a huge amount of money. I'll have to ask a few people first …'

The point is that those who did talk about death were quite practical about it, for the most part. More practical, perhaps, than us young 'uns. I'd be tempted to venture that they hope they get old before they die. Neat, but wrong. They don't see age as relevant and there isn't a tidy song for that.

John Reilly's ceremony will be a simple one. I hope it won't take place for a long, long time. When it does, it promises to be impressive. Its story starts in the late eighties. John, former minder to Judy Garland, former assistant to R.D. Laing, eventually became a psychotherapist and counsellor. But he decided to take a sabbatical from psychotherapy – something professionals are encouraged to do for their own mental health. At the time, the late eighties, he was involved with a lady who didn't drink or do drugs. 'We were having fantastic sex every day and I decided I would follow her example.' So he took a sabbatical from alcohol and drugs. He didn't find this difficult, despite the fact he had taken on a managerial post at the Portobello Gold public house.

He had already hired a drama student to work behind the bar, and she told John she had a friend, another drama student, who needed a job. The friend duly showed up, was OK'd by John and he set to work. But at the end of the shift, John found him on the doorstep of the Gold, suitcase at his feet, looking disconsolate. He was homeless and skint. John offered him houseroom. He stayed a year. They became friends, despite the age difference. Because of the age difference, maybe. The drama student didn't pay rent. No need. John didn't ask. They remain friends. The drama student agreed, jokily, to read the tribute to John at his funeral.

In my mind's eye, it's packed with Groovy Old Men and, while they wait, the keen-eared among them notice that it's 'Hotel California' they're hearing, subtly rendered into an organ fugue. John loves The Eagles. But as they sit, they're hushed by a replacement soundtrack, something sixties, ultra-recognisable. And up the aisle comes John's friend from the Gold days, immaculate in Paul Smith. A lot of the mourners are wearing Paul Smith. Including Paul Smith. But why this musical theme? As John's friend turns to face us, it becomes clear. It's the James Bond theme and Paul's friend, the skint guy on the doorstep of the pub, the guy he adopted, is Daniel Craig.

At my request, Daniel is contacted on the set of the latest 007 movie. Daniel laughs and says diplomatically that he'll have to bow out, because one of John's sons wants to do the honours. I don't want to hijack the event. Anyway, this should be about life, not death.

Bond would be the perfect icon, though. Or patron saint. Not afraid to be self-indulgent, vain even, but modest with it, a man who started his history in the fifties and the Cold War, but is capable of Gallifreyan renewal. OK, he's no rock 'n' roller, but his sig tune has endured for over 40 years. Not a Groovy Old Man himself (too young), but a lasting icon to the Groovy Old Man community. Some of the actors who've played him *are* Groovy Old Men, of course: Sean Connery certainly; Roger Moore, not so sure. Whatever happened to George Lazenby? And are we judging the character here, or the actor?

Come on, you've read the book, now play the game. Jack Nicholson, certainly. But he's a film star. And he's American. David Bailey …? That bloke in the chemist, you know, the one with the ears … is he old enough? James Dyson, invented the thingamy, the *Dyson* … how old's he, then? Clive James. Charlie Watts. That teacher we had … your dad … no, *your* dad …

* * * * *

No Groovy Old Men were hurt in the making of this book. Hurt no, offended, possibly. Some didn't like the word 'Groovy'. Some were a bit iffy about 'Old', and one, Paulette the Tart, might have taken issue with the 'Man'.

I'd also like to pay tribute to the ones that got away. The man with the thick glasses, leather hat and funny beard in a suburban Marks & Spencer, peering very closely at, I think, coleslaw; the tall black guy with the grey dreadlocks in Lewisham, south-east London; a kind of hip Father Christmas-looking chap having a smoke yesterday outside an antiques shop in a small town in Kent; the 80-year-old academic with the much younger wife and the newly acquired taste in scuba diving; the Irishman with the ice cream parlour who dated Diana Dors; the man who stole Gram Parsons' corpse (although he's American and may not count); anyone over 60 flying a kite by themselves; 40 per cent of the audience who went to see the Bonzos at the Astoria in June 2008; 27 per cent of the audience for the Stones movie *Shine a Light*; and all the frightened-looking blokes I stopped in the streets who looked Groovy but declined to take part.

London, June 2008

ACKNOWLEDGEMENTS

With special thanks to Nigel Acheson, who just had time to provide duffel coat data; Clive Brill for the Doubting Thomas, Najma Finlay for the bad boys, Jane Firth, Ian Gardhouse, Elisa and Pete McAuley, Polly Prattent, Brian King, Michael Magenis, Zoe Meads, Nick Parker, Mark Pettigrew, Martin Plimmer, Caroline Raphael, Alison Vernon Smith, Steve Shepherd, Lore Windemuth, Dr Paul Wolfson and all the Groovy Old Men and possibly women I talked to. Thanks too to my patient editor, Duncan Heath.